MY Outback CHILDHOOD

MY Outback CHILDHOOD

Growing up in the Territory

TONI TAPP COUTTS

With best wishes from Australia
Toni Tapp Coutts

LOTHIAN   2019

People of Aboriginal or Torres Strait Islander heritage are advised that this book contains the names of people who are deceased or may be deceased.

A Lothian Children's Book

Published in Australia and New Zealand in 2018
by Hachette Australia
(an imprint of Hachette Australia Pty Limited)
Level 17, 207 Kent Street, Sydney NSW 2000
www.hachettechildrens.com.au

10 9 8 7 6 5 4 3 2 1

Text copyright © Toni Tapp Coutts 2018

This book is copyright. Apart from any fair dealing for the purposes of private study, research, criticism or review permitted under the *Copyright Act 1968*, no part may be stored or reproduced by any process without prior written permission. Enquiries should be made to the publisher.

 A catalogue record for this book is available from the National Library of Australia

ISBN 978 0 7344 1833 3 (paperback)

Cover design by Luke Causby/Blue Cork
Cover photograph courtesy of Toni Tapp Coutts
Author photo courtesy of Jodie Bilske
Text design by Bookhouse, Sydney
Typeset in 12/17.3 pt Adobe Garamond Pro by Bookhouse, Sydney
Printed and bound in Australia by McPherson's Printing Group

 The paper this book is printed on is certified against the Forest Stewardship Council® Standards. McPherson's Printing Group holds FSC® chain of custody certification SA-COC-005379. FSC® promotes environmentally responsible, socially beneficial and economically viable management of the world's forests.

My childhood was spent taking care of my brothers and sisters, playing with my friends and falling in love with the land I grew up on. I was happy on Killarney. I couldn't imagine a better place to live, or a better life to lead, even if to most people's way of thinking it would have seemed as though we had nothing.

That 'nothing' was rich with love and adventure.
It was everything!

Contents

Introduction ix

1 Alice Springs and Me 1
2 Katherine 4
3 My New Dad 11
4 Our New Home 18
5 Aboriginal People on Killarney 24
6 Everyday Life on Killarney 32
7 Seasons in the Northern Territory 39
8 Hunting with Dora and Daisy 46
9 Bush Tucker 53
10 Kids' Games 60
11 Where's the Water? 68
12 Family Life 73
13 Animal Antics 78
14 Killarney Grows Bigger and Bigger 85

15	Monsters from the Deep and Other Stories	93
16	Killarney's Cattle	99
17	The Cattle Yards and Our Head Stockman	105
18	Communicating with the Outside World	112
19	Raining Fish and Life in the Wet	117
20	Camping	125
21	Accidents Happen	131
22	A Bush Education	137
23	Our Own Governess	143
24	Boarding School Days	148
25	Killarney Now	156

Glossary 159

Acknowledgements 163

Introduction

Hi. My name is Toni Tapp Coutts and the story you're about to read is a real one. It's about how I grew up with my nine siblings on a cattle station in the Northern Territory. I always knew I wanted to write my story because I realised my childhood was quite different to a lot of other Australian kids' childhoods growing up at that time.

A lot has changed since I was little, but I know there are still hundreds of kids around Australia attending classes through School of the Air in remote locations, growing up in similar circumstances to the way my brothers and sisters and I did.

For everyone who reads this, whether you live in a brick house and attend a big school in the city, or you live on a farm with sheep or cows for company in the bush, I hope that you enjoy the many stories of the ups and downs my family and I had living on the beautiful, harsh and rich land that was Killarney Cattle Station.

1 Alice Springs and Me

In 1955, I was born smack bang in the middle of the country, in a dusty desert town called Alice Springs in outback Australia. The hot, harsh climate in the centre of the country has a roller-coaster of temperatures ranging from minus seven to a super-hot 45 degrees Celsius. It's where kangaroos, wallabies, mulga snakes and the occasional thorny devil have made their home for thousands of years.

The red desert in Central Australia is as flat as a pancake, with mountain ranges popping up at intervals to create ancient gorges that whisper the stories of the Indigenous Arrernte people who have walked the land for the last 40 000 years. The sky is a million light years away and yet, at night, feels so close you could just stretch your hand and touch the Milky Way.

The Aboriginal name for Alice Springs is Mparntwe. Back when I was born, the Aboriginal people lived on the banks of the Todd River at the fringes of town in humpies made from paperbark trees and scraps of rusty corrugated iron. They were forbidden to live together with white people.

At the time of my birth, Alice Springs had been gripped by a devastating drought for ten years and red sand hills were piled around the town, right up to our front door, covering suburban fences, roads and footpaths, old cars and gardens. Alice Springs was a tough place for anyone to live in. With a population of just 1500, it was a simple outback town without television or telephones, where few families had washing machines or a family car.

My mum named me Toni because she loved a Hollywood actor called Anthony Quinn. She loved to tell me the story that on her first day out shopping after my birth, she left me asleep in the pram at the butcher shop while she caught a taxi home. She arrived back at the house with the groceries and no baby, so she had to return to town in the taxi to pick me up – finding me none the worse for wear, fast asleep in the corner!

My brother Billy was born in December 1957 and my baby sister Shing two years after that, in August 1960. Billy and I slept in the one bed and Shing in a rickety wooden cot. Shing's official name is Kristen; however, she was called 'Little Thing', which became 'Little Shing', and that finally became Shing. Shing was a tiny thing who sucked her thumb and everyone loved her, including me.

I spent the first five years of my life in Alice Springs, but I think my real adventure began once Mum took Billy, Shing and me with her further north, back to Katherine to live with her mum. Although our dad stayed behind, he had never been a big part of our lives and I don't remember missing him. Our mum, June, was everything to us, and as long as she was going somewhere new, we'd be going with her. She'd decided she didn't want to stay in Alice with her husband, and that her life was going in a different direction, which meant my life was about to change in a big way too.

2 Katherine

In 1960 it wasn't easy for a woman to leave a marriage, especially a mother with three small children. There were no government or welfare benefits to support women if they left. The men controlled all the finances and did not have to support the family.

Mum didn't receive any payments to help her with living costs. She packed everything she needed into a couple of suitcases and, along with her three babies, flew the 1200 kilometres north to live with her mother, Gladys, in Katherine.

I loved living with my nana. The house was full of people coming and going, so there were always extra people at the dinner table and plenty of laughter.

The town's European history started when an explorer named John McDouall Stuart found himself in the area in 1862 and he named the Katherine River after the daughter of John Chambers, a wealthy South Australian landowner who helped finance Stuart's exploration of the north. In the 1960s it was still home to the local Aboriginal people, the Jawoyn, Dagoman, Dalabon and Wardaman peoples, and about 300 white people. It was a busy, vibrant town with a dusty main street and a railway station that serviced the massive outback region from Darwin to Birdum, just south of Katherine. Katherine has always owed much of its livelihood – and its recent history – to the pastoral industry and the railway.

Katherine's streets were full of the red dirt that is typical of that part of Australia. It gets on cars and people, and is embedded into the asphalt on the roads. The red landscape is punctuated by large frangipani trees covered in deep green leaves and small clusters of blossoms; there are poincianas with their flame-red flowers and mango trees laden with heavy fruit, and lots of other tropical trees that provide homes and shelter for all sorts of insects and animals.

In the dry season the searing heat of the day is barely broken at night and in the wet season the whole region grows lush and heavy with humidity. While I was growing up, air conditioning hadn't been invented and the best we could hope for was a ceiling fan to shift the air around, although it didn't make it much cooler. The dirt, the heat and humidity were just facts of life.

When we moved to Katherine it had a post office, two pubs, a hospital, police station and church. There were two garages and two cafes, along with Cox's Store and Katherine Stores, both owned by the Cox family. There was a picture theatre in the main street where the white people sat in canvas chairs up the back and the Aboriginal people sat on a cement slab with their blankets at the front. There was a tin roof over the seated area that leaked buckets of water when it rained, the noise drowning out the sounds of the movie.

The factory where my grandmother worked was a huge, noisy corrugated-iron shed right next door to her house. Nana's best friends owned the factory. Nana worked long hours making the fizzy soft drinks that we called lolly water, so we used to say that she worked at the lolly water factory. I thought it was pretty special that Nana worked there, because lolly water was such a treat – and she had access to it every single day!

Nana's job was to load the thick cordial base into the machines. The bottles rattled along conveyor belts and were filled with bubbling soda water, then topped up with sticky, sweet, coloured syrups. The bottles were then juggled along another large clunking machine where the caps were clamped onto them. They were manually packed into wooden crates and delivered to the local shops. There was sarsaparilla, raspberry, orange, lemonade, lime, creaming soda, banana, pineapple, cola, ginger ale and ginger beer, and large quantities of plain soda water.

The factory later supplied shops with the specially designed soft-drink fridges that allowed you to insert a coin into the slot in the side of the machine to release the cold drink. These were very modern pieces of equipment for a town that didn't have telephones or televisions. The shops would clean the empty soft-drink bottles, put them into the crates and return them to the factory, where they were placed into vats of caustic soda for a final clean and then refilled with lolly water.

In 1969, the lolly water factory was bought from the Scott family by my uncle Jim Forscutt, who expanded the business to supply soft drinks as far away as the mining town of Tennant Creek and the roadhouses of Barry Caves to the south and Adelaide River in the north.

When Nana started working at the factory my grandfather Nick was still alive, but he had died before we moved to Katherine, so I never knew him.

An Aboriginal couple, Maudie and Smiler, helped Nana with the children, the washing and looking after the garden. I suppose our arrival in Katherine just meant more people for Nana to look after, as Mum's three younger brothers and sister were there as well as our Great Uncle

Bill, plus there were friends, and friends of friends who stayed for weeks and months at a time. But we all fitted into the old corrugated-iron house with its rough cement floors and rickety doors that were never closed. There was plenty of room for everyone at the big wooden kitchen table where we gathered at lunchtime to listen to the ABC radio news and a long-running radio serial called *Blue Hills*.

My nana's house was pretty basic, with a big hot water 'donkey' out the back of the laundry. This donkey was a 44-gallon drum set on four metal 'legs', with a fire lit under it to boil the water for the house. We liked climbing through the woodheap full of snakes to gather wood to stoke the fire. The bedrooms at one end of the house were separated by curtains strung on fencing wire from steel beams. Large, wispy, white mosquito nets flowed over the wrought-iron beds with their bumpy mattresses. The beds were high off the floor and wooden soft-drink crates were kept underneath so we could climb up into bed.

I hated going to the corrugated-iron toilet down the backyard. The toilet itself, made from a cut-out 44-gallon drum, was too high for small children, so we had to climb up onto the seat and squat over the hole, which revealed a massive black glob of poo mixed with the magazines and newspapers that were used as toilet paper. In the hot weather the stench was horrible!

The rickety door was heavy and didn't close properly either. The tin walls were recycled roofing iron that was dotted with nail holes to peek through and see if anyone was coming. The spider webs rustled around your ears and the toilet creaked in the wind and sighed with the heat. I was terrified of the toilet at night, because I knew that not only were there snakes, lizards, frogs and goannas but also a scary boogie man who would kidnap me, for sure. There seemed to be boogie men everywhere in Katherine, as my little friends and I were always hiding from them under the beds in the house or when playing games in the huge mango trees. Happily, I never saw a boogie man!

It was a happy, rowdy house where my teenage uncle and aunt and their friends practised rock 'n' roll dancing to a bumpy record player in the lounge room. The rough, pitted cement floor did not stop them from rehearsing their routines over and over. I thought Aunty Sue was a movie star with her gorgeous blonde hair, as she twirled in her large skirts and fancy shoes under Uncle Jim's arms and around his body; changing direction in the blink of an eye, she slipped under his legs and spun around and around, skirts swishing up to her thighs. Uncle Jim was a lovable, boisterous and bumptious character, and he called my grandmother 'Tango' when he was in a cheeky mood.

There was never a dull moment at Nana's house for me, Billy or Shing. There were so many people there at times it felt as though we were being raised by a village – and we liked it that way. It was good for Mum too, to have lots of people around to help with us kids. If she ever had a moment of missing our father we would never have known.

3 My New Dad

The first time I saw Bill Tapp I was five years old and he was standing in the doorway of my nana's house. He was hard to miss: he stood six feet and two inches, sported a big black moustache and a ten-gallon hat, dark moleskin trousers, a blue long-sleeved shirt and riding boots. Around his hips he had two leather belts – one a bull strap for catching wild bulls and the other a bandolier with a row of silver bullets – and a black Luger pistol jutting out of a holster, just like in the cowboy movies.

No wonder my mother fell for him straightaway.

It was 1960 and Bill Tapp had come to town with my two uncles, who worked for him at Killarney Station. They invited him to stay at my grandmother's house whenever he was in town.

'Hello, M-M-Mrrrsss F-F-F-Forscutt,' Bill Tapp would stutter in his deep voice. He always called her 'M-M-Mrrrsss F-F-F-Forscutt' no matter how many times she said, 'Oh, Bill, for goodness' sake, call me Glad.'

Katherine did not have a motel or boarding hostel at that time, so anyone who was visiting town had to find someone to stay with. More often than not, it seemed, that someone was Nana. She always had a meal and a bed out the back for the boarders who would come and stay for as long as they needed to.

Born Charles William Tapp in Sydney in June 1929, Bill Tapp was an only child. The Tapps lived in a grand, sprawling house with a tennis court and a housekeeper. Bill Tapp never lost his taste for the finer things in life. He attended a private school, The Scots College, in Bellevue Hill. In his senior years at school Bill Tapp became a full-time boarder, as his father was ill with cancer and his mother travelled overseas for her work buying homewares. Bill Tapp was good at everything he applied himself to, representing his school in swimming, rowing, cricket, boxing and football. He played tennis with Australian champions Ken Rosewall, Lew Hoad and Frank Sedgman during his school years. Though tall and good looking as a teenager, and accomplished at so many things, self-confidence was not one of Bill Tapp's strong points. He was shy and the stutter that was evident when we met him in Katherine would stay with him all his life.

His lifelong schoolfriend was David Brockhoff, who went on to become one of Australia's great rugby union identities, playing eight Tests as flanker between 1949 and 1951. He also coached the Australian team for several years in the 1970s.

Bill Tapp's life in the Northern Territory was completely different to his Sydney upbringing. It began as an idea when, as a teenager, he read the book *The Cattle King* by Ion L. Idriess, the story of Sir Sidney Kidman, who had started with almost nothing after running away from home at the age of thirteen and ended up owning an empire of cattle stations across the north of Australia.

Although Bill Tapp had a comfortable life, there was clearly something about this story that clicked with him. Most of his school holidays were spent with his school mates who had cattle and horse properties in country New South Wales. A friend from those days said Bill Tapp immediately had a rapport with the animals and quickly became a good horseman and confident in handling livestock.

Bill Tapp wrote to his mother from boarding school, telling her that he wanted to leave Sydney as soon as he finished school to go to the Northern Territory. By chance, his mother had met a Mr H.E. Thonemann, who owned the sprawling, isolated cattle property Elsey Station in the Northern Territory, near the tiny township of Mataranka, 400 kilometres south of Darwin; Elsey Station was made famous by Jeannie Gunn in her book, *We of the Never Never*. Young Bill got a job as a jackaroo–bookkeeper, starting at Elsey Station in 1947.

Bill Tapp soon settled into station life, learning everything he could, and the manager and his wife looked after him well. Bill Tapp said to me much later that when he arrived at Elsey Station he was upset to discover the difference in conditions between the white workers and the Aboriginals. The Aboriginal people lived in humpies and were dished out limited food and tobacco for smoking, with no access to toilets, showers or a laundry to wash their clothes, and they were not invited to eat anywhere near the white people. He'd never experienced anything like it and he didn't like the injustice of it. He felt it wasn't fair, even though he lived in only slightly better conditions, a shed when he was at the station and swags most of the time. He thought the Aboriginal people should be treated the same as him.

After a few years at Elsey Station, he and his boss began their own droving business in the early 1950s, moving cattle from Alice Springs through Tennant Creek and Elliott and along the Murranji Track to the Kimberley in Western Australia. The Murranji, one of the most notoriously treacherous stock routes in the Northern Territory, was known for its long distances between waterholes through hot, dry lancewood country. The drovers needed to have a very good knowledge of the distances, the pace they could push the cattle and what waterholes would still have water by the end of the dry season.

By 1960, Bill Tapp was able to buy his own cattle station, his childhood dream come true. For the sum of £90 000, a record price for a Northern Territory cattle station at that time, he became the proud owner of Killarney. This gave him the freedom to implement and develop his own ideas and plans – his transformation into a Territory cattle king was now underway. The signing over of the property took some time but this did not stop Bill Tapp from working day and night, mustering and building fences to contain the wild cattle that roamed the area. He finally received the title to Killarney in 1962.

Bill Tapp's empire began under a bough shed at Mayvale Bore on Killarney. He led a frugal life, working with a stock camp that consisted of my teenage uncles and three other young men. They slept in swags, moving around the station with pack horses carrying their swags, shoeing and fencing gear and all the supplies, and their food – flour, salted beef, sugar and tea. They rarely went to town or indulged in luxuries such as a warm shower or a beer.

Bill Tapp told my uncles that he fell in love with my mother the first day he saw her, and that he was going to marry her. He was thirty-one years old by then and he had never had a girlfriend – which was hardly a surprise, given the life he'd been leading: there weren't many unmarried women to be found on the cattle stations of the Northern Territory.

Their relationship developed quickly over a very short period of time. Bill Tapp's idea of dating was to take Mum to the river and show off his diving skills by doing swan dives and backflips off the Low Level bridge into the Katherine River, while us kids paddled around in the shallows. He was a man of few words and didn't talk much to us; however, I immediately liked and trusted him because I felt the intense love that he had for my mother. He also liked Nana and her no-nonsense family, who were some of the few who could draw him out of his shyness with a good joke and a big laugh. He seemed keen to take on the whole package of a ready-made family.

We had a big extended family around us and lots of new little friends in the neighbourhood. I felt secure and happy in my life, and I am sure Billy and Shing felt the same. We had no reason to worry about anything – we had family and fun every day of our lives, and we were well taken care of. Bill Tapp was just another interesting addition to our full lives.

From very early on, he was always called 'Bill Tapp'. Everyone called him 'Bill Tapp'. None of the children ever called him 'Dad' – in later years I would sometimes tease him and call him 'Dad', but he would grow uncomfortable and gruffly say, 'Bill Tapp,' in response.

Before long, Bill Tapp asked my mother to go out to Killarney with him. He wanted to marry her, and in 1961 we were making plans to drive the 270 kilometres to Killarney.

As far as Billy and I were concerned, this was just another adventure. Shing was far too young to know what was going on. The three of us were a little pack and we would follow Mum wherever she went. We were leaving Nana and her boisterous household behind but she wouldn't be far away. A new life was waiting for us down a road that we would come to travel many times over the next few years.

4 Our New Home

When my mother asked Bill Tapp what she needed to take for her first trip out to Killarney cattle station, he replied, 'Oh, don't worry, we have everything we need.'

In her excitement at going bush and living in a real homestead, my mother packed only the necessities: a small suitcase of clothing, tins of powdered milk and baby bottles, Weet-Bix, tins of Heinz baked beans and spaghetti, and lots of nappies. Mum was cautious but also head over heels in love with Bill Tapp and prepared to take on whatever was waiting for her at this strange new place. She never thought about the consequences of what she was doing; she never considered that life at Killarney might be considerably different to life in Katherine. She's always been pretty adventurous.

On that first trip to Killarney we travelled all day. It was a hot, dusty drive over scratchy dirt tracks, up rocky ridges, down dry creeks and across black soil plains; my mother and Bill Tapp were cramped with three children in the front seat of a smoke-blowing, engine-roaring Bedford truck.

The miles crept slowly by; we pulled over now and then for a toilet stop, to stretch our legs and have a drink of water before finally arriving beside a creaking windmill and rusty water tank just as the sun was going down. After almost 300 kilometres, Mum crawled out of the truck, exhausted, and let the children out to have a run around.

'How much further do we have to go?' she asked Bill Tapp.

'Oh, this is it,' he proudly declared as he pointed to a bough shed with no walls and an open fire surrounded by black pots and pans. Mum stared in amazement at her new home: a rickety shed made of six wooden posts with dried tree branches layered over the top for a roof.

There wasn't much else at Killarney besides that shed. The area around Mayvale Bore was almost without trees, as they'd been cut down by the previous occupants for use as firewood. The ground was dry, and the flat red landscape was dotted with millions of ant hills, scrawny trees and stumpy yellow grass as far as the eye could see. And out there, somewhere, were cattle. It was Bill Tapp's dream to fill Killarney with proper cattle yards, camp buildings and a homestead. That vision was still in his head, though – all we could see when we arrived was an almost empty area around the shed, and beyond that the bare land stretching away on all sides.

When Mum asked Bill Tapp where the toilet was, he said, 'Down the creek.' She set off on foot with Billy, Shing and me, looking for a lone tin shed. After quite a trek with no sign of anything that looked like a toilet except the odd scattering of newspaper and toilet paper littered along the dry riverbed, she realised that the 'toilet' was to squat behind the biggest tree you could find.

Bill Tapp had told Mum that 'everything they needed' was at Killarney but what he really meant was 'everything a man needed' – that is, swags under a tree, and plenty of beef, flour, sugar and black tea.

There was a large open fire with buckets of water and cast-iron camp ovens simmering away on the coals – for cooking and, when needed, for keeping warm – and a massive woodheap full of insects and snakes. Damper, which is bread made from flour, baking powder, salt and water, large slabs of roast beef and stews were cooked in those camp ovens, which were put in a hole in the ground with hot stones placed in the bottom and hot coals on the top. There were billycans filled with thick black tea and the camp ovens were moved about by using cooking utensils that were shaped out of fencing wire. There was no house, no running water or refrigeration, no toilet or fresh food or vegetables. My mother might not have been used to living in luxury but she had never lived out in the open before – let alone subjected her children to such conditions.

Mum quickly learnt to sleep in a swag on the ground, to do the washing in cut-off 44-gallon drums and bathe the three of us in tin buckets behind the water tank. We soon adapted to having no proper toilet – when you're a little kid, a thing like that isn't a big deal.

The bough shed was the kitchen, the office and doctor's surgery all at once. Communications with the outside world were conducted on a two-way radio that was powered by a twelve-volt battery. The radio sat on a rusty five-gallon drum under a tree with its wire aerial thrown into the branches in search of patchy atmospheric reception. The 'scheds' – scheduled sessions – were the set times designated to send telegrams and order food, stores and mechanical parts for the station, to have inter-station discussions with neighbours, to buy and sell cattle, or talk to the doctor. These calls were transferred through Radio Victor Juliet Yankee (VJY) from Wyndham in Western Australia, three times a day. Most of the time the radio was crackly and indecipherable but everyone knew everyone's business anyway. Announcements of births, marriages and deaths were also transmitted across the airwaves.

There was no electricity, no telephones, or television, so when we weren't tearing about the place we entertained ourselves with storytelling, guitars and music – we were never bored. My mother was reliant on drovers travelling through the area to bring supplies of powdered milk, tinned vegetables and the most treasured items: old newspapers, magazines and books. Mum loved to read and worked her way through most of the world's classic novels thanks to what the drovers gave her when they passed through. She would say that she knew the instructions on the milk and jam tins off by heart because if there was nothing else to read, she read the labels. Bill Tapp loved to read *Queensland Country Life* and *Phantom* comics. He kept a diary and journalled the wages and stores in a red hardcover book.

There were about fifteen people living on the outstation at this time. Because there was no housing, everyone camped under humpies or tarpaulins strung between trees.

My mother, Bill Tapp and we three kids slept in open swags under our chandelier of stars. Our swags were thin, itchy, grey army blankets and the pillows were made of the sum total of our clothing rolled into a little bundle. Sleeping like this for me was just normal – everyone else was sleeping in a swag, so it didn't occur to me to miss the bed I'd known in Nana's house in Katherine.

Under the Milky Way we held competitions to see who was the first to spot the Evening Star, who was the first to find a satellite floating steadily across the galaxy and who saw the first sliver of moon break onto the southern horizon.

From a very young age, I could identify the Southern Cross and Orion with his belt and scabbard. I loved the full-moon nights when the shadows of the trees turned into scary monsters with which I could create stories of monsters and boogie men to frighten my younger siblings. On moonless nights we curled up with the blankets over our heads in case those boogie men came to get us. During the wet season we shared our shelter – an upturned water tank – with spiders and snakes all trying to get out of the rain.

I was happy, sitting around the open campfire for breakfast and dinner with Mum, Bill Tapp and the stockmen, and running wild with my brother Billy. The men went mustering all day, so while they were gone there was mostly just my mother, and the Aboriginal women Daisy and Dora, who entertained us with songs and stories, and took us hunting for bush tucker. We were all burnt brown because we ran around in pants with no shoes or shirts. Our knotted hair was full of nits. It was a very free way of living – if we didn't wear clothes there weren't clothes to get dirty, so Mum didn't have to wash as much, which was fine by us.

5 Aboriginal People on Killarney

Before we moved to Killarney, a passing drover had told Bill Tapp about a small group of Aboriginal people walking around the country who were looking for work. They were living in the scrub, away from their homelands, and no one would give them a job. Bill Tapp eventually tracked down the small family and offered them a job.

The Aboriginal families who lived on Killarney were mainly Mudburra people, with inter-family connections to the Gurindji people of Wave Hill. One of the Aboriginal women, Dora, lived under a humpy with her daughter Nita, who was a couple of years older than me, while another woman, Daisy, and her husband, Banjo – who was Dora's son – camped just a short way from them. The single Aboriginal men, Georgie and Cloud, camped further away under another tree. The white stockmen camped with their mates from Katherine further away from the women.

Banjo Long, who was known to be a good cattleman, had the reputation of being a wild warrior who had killed a couple of Aboriginal men in inter-clan feuds, and had assaulted a white police officer from Timber Creek when they attempted to arrest him. He was known as the Rain Man because he could sing for rain. His wife, Daisy, was a large, cuddly lady with a very sweet personality. His brother Georgie was wire thin and agile with a lovely wide smile; he was always happy.

Georgie made boomerangs, woomeras and long spears with deadly ironwood points. He loved to show off his boomerang-throwing skills by setting up a flour drum as a target for his practice. He performed the moves of the brolga and kangaroo dances, and did all sorts of bird calls. He taught me how to blow a leaf and make songs as we rode along behind mobs of cattle.

Dora was the boss woman in the camp. We called her Mum and everyone else called her 'Old Dora'. She was a small, round lady who had one deformed foot with three funny little toes bunched together. She wrapped a big bundle of rags, torn grey blankets and a hessian bag around the foot to build it up. The bundle of old rags and blankets was held together with a long piece of cord wrapped around and around the bag. The cord was made from strips of fabric torn from old dresses, knotted together and rolled in goanna fat to give it strength.

Dora got about easily on her bag foot, as we called it, and could keep up with the strongest of us as we walked up and down creek beds and across rocky ridges. The crippled foot never slowed her down. She was a strong and wiry traditional woman who walked the length and breadth of the Northern Territory and had given birth to ten children.

During her time on Killarney, Dora was a cranky old woman who ruled the camp with her tongue and a nulla nulla, a type of fighting stick. She was the oldest person in her small group and did not have a husband when she came to Killarney – although she must have had one once, given that she had ten children! Old Dora's word was law and I never saw anyone attempt to challenge her, even her big, strong son Banjo.

Dora taught us the order of Aboriginal society according to skin names and relationships. Skin names are a complicated system created by Aboriginal people over the millennia to ensure that there are no close family bloodline marriages within the small tribes. Dora took us into her family and we took her family into ours. She gave my mother a tribal skin name of the Mudburra and Gurindji people, Nunaku, which made them sisters. Through these skin names we were Dora's children, which made Banjo and his brother Georgie my brothers. My skin name (and my sisters') is Ngunnarryi and the boys' name is Djungarri.

I became proficient in speaking pidgin English smattered with the local Mudburra and Gurindji dialect and a library full of useful swear words. Dora also painted us with ochre and taught us dances and songs. She told us about the Dreaming and drew animal tracks and stories in the dirt. She taught us all about bush tucker and medicine.

Daisy was a bit younger than Dora. We called her 'Buggadu', Gurindji language for 'auntie' or 'sister-in-law'; because Banjo was our brother, we had to call Daisy 'sister-in-law', even though she was old enough to be our grandmother.

The young Aboriginal girls on Killarney were not allowed to look at or talk to Banjo or Georgie, as was the traditional practice through the skin system in which the women are not allowed to interact with their brothers or speak their names aloud.

Everyone liked Daisy; she was kind and gentle. She sang corroboree songs in a high, sweet voice and told us stories about the Dreaming that coexisted with and ruled their day-to-day lives. Daisy did all the work because she was Dora's daughter-in-law. She prepared the food: rib bones, goanna and little johnnycakes, a type of flat bread made with flour, baking powder, salt and water, pummelled into a flat round cake and cooked on the open coals. She cooked beautiful golden loaves of bread in camp ovens and made brooms out of bushes tied to a long stick to rake the ground around the camp. She did the washing and made huge dresses and petticoats out of cheap floral material, sewing in tiny running stitches with black cotton.

We kids would play under the overflow of the tank and make mud pies while the old women bathed in a cut-off petrol drum behind the water tank. They did their washing at the same time and hung it on a barbed-wire fence to dry. They wore handmade half-slips and their breasts hung free. They had deep tribal scars on their upper arms and they painted lines and circle symbols on their long breasts with white ochre.

All of this seemed normal to me: it was how they lived and it was what I grew up with. Daisy and Dora bathed, oiled their skin and wore their best dresses and scarves when they went down to the corrugated-tin store that my mother ran.

The Aboriginal residents were provided with a weekly box of stores that consisted of flour, baking powder, salt, sugar, tins of jam and treacle, washing soap and tobacco. They collected their rations and carried everything home tied in a strip of cloth.

Clothing, bedding and all personal items such as soap, shampoo and medicines were ordered from Katherine as needed.

These were the times before Aboriginal people were able to legally drink or buy alcohol, when clap sticks and didgeridoos played through the night at the camp. This was also the time of segregation, pre-1967 when Aboriginal people were given the vote. It was against the law for a white person to cohabit with or marry an Aboriginal person. The result was the Stolen Generation, a law that forcibly removed children of mixed blood from their predominantly Aboriginal mothers and placed them into orphanages and church-run institutions.

The Aboriginal people had a keen sense of humour and would joke and laugh among themselves. It was a sense of humour that most people would not understand until you got to know them well. They loved to send each other up and would laugh at one another's mishaps and blunders, such as being a bit too slow to get out of the way of a cow, or falling off a horse.

They kept their strict family protocols in rapidly changing times. Tensions did rise to the surface at times as people from different cultures and different countries lived in Killarney's small community. There was an incident when Banjo, Georgie and another Aboriginal man named Martin protested about having to do 'women's work': Bill

Tapp had made them cart water in buckets up to their women in the Aboriginal camp.

In protest, the men put on dresses and tied red scarves around their heads and carried the water, two buckets full, slung on the end of a stick across their shoulders, just as the women did. While it was considered a bit of a joke, it was also a serious statement that these men did not do women's work and the women should, and would, carry the water themselves. The men were not asked to carry buckets of water in the same fashion as the women again – they could deliver the water on the back of a vehicle in drums instead. This was different, and acceptable, because the men could drive, and driving was not considered a woman's job.

I asked my mother once how she felt about living with traditional people who spoke little English. She said, 'I was never lonely. I was quite surprised to find this sense of humour in Aboriginal people because, like most white people, I treated them seriously. As I got to know them I saw them as ordinary people, just surviving, living and laughing like everyone else. They laughed at all the things that I found amusing, which is a little bit of a putdown of other people, or finding other people's pretensions amusing. They were very perceptive about white people's self-importance and could mimic them very quickly. Old Dora in particular was very perceptive, whereas Old Daisy was more the gentle giant.'

During the first years at Killarney, the Aboriginal Affairs Department paid the cattle station owners forty cents a week welfare payment as compensation to the pastoralist to support an adult Aboriginal woman and her child. It was the expectation that the station provided everything to the large extended family of the Aboriginal stockmen. This included all food, clothing and housing. We were all living in third-world conditions and with little income that came in sporadically on the delivery of a truckload of bulls to the meatworks. My mother told the department: 'We are all living on the smell of an oily rag – how are we expected to maintain an adult person on forty cents a week? It costs forty cents for a cup of coffee in town.'

Mum was a great mentor to the Aboriginal women, trying to lift their health standards and get the kids to school. She wanted everyone to achieve in life and never held anyone back, whether they were her own kids or other people in the camp. We were all in it together.

We all, black and white, lived in the same harsh conditions with poor housing and sanitation, water shortages, and lack of decent food, while working long hours in extreme weather conditions. We were also working towards a common goal: making life easier for everyone who lived at Killarney.

6 Everyday Life on Killarney

Bill Tapp was a workaholic and perfectionist, and he expected everyone around him to be the same. The men who worked for him were given a Sunday morning off to do their washing and the only other breaks taken were to attend the Katherine Show or the Victoria River Downs Races. In return they were given an annual pay cheque and everything they needed to live while they were on Killarney.

The conditions might sound harsh, but when you don't have to worry about where you're going to sleep or how you're going to eat, life is a lot less stressful. These men worked hard, for sure, but Bill Tapp also took his responsibilities towards them — towards all of us — seriously.

In August 1962, my mum and Bill Tapp got married and three weeks later my brother Sam was born. The living conditions on Killarney were hardly kind to the mother of a newborn, let alone one who already had three children to deal with. For one thing, the little black bush flies were relentless. They clung to the corners of our eyes and mouths to suck out every skerrick of moisture. They covered our backs in a dark mass, like a swarming blanket. They bombarded our food and we had to lift them out of our pannikins of tea. They ate the soft flesh around the cattle's eyes. We kids also had constant bung eyes and boils. Moreover, there were always thousands of black ants in the food – but no one bothered about them, we just picked them out and kept on eating.

Snakes, goannas, spiders, ants and lizards were regular visitors looking for warmth in our swags, along with the odd mad cow stamping through the campfire, knocking over tables and drums of flour, and ripping the tent cover, looking for water.

Mum was terrified of snakes, cattle, dogs and horses – she never learnt to ride. There wasn't much on Killarney that didn't scare her. She would scream out, 'Bill, Bill, there's a snake in the swag!' as she scooped up the baby in her arms and backed away, trying to keep an eye on the unwelcome visitor. Each time there was a snake nearby, my brother Billy and I loved to go into battle with a long stick, as Mum yelled, 'Get out of the way, you kids! Get out of the way!' Her cries did little to deter us. Probably we were a bit silly, because we didn't realise how dangerous those snakes could be. None of us ever got bitten, though, so maybe the long sticks did their job.

The 2819 square kilometres of bush that was Killarney Station was my playground and I loved every inch of it. There was always something interesting around every corner, be it a fat, juicy bush turkey that ended up on the campfire for dinner, brumbies and wild donkeys disappearing through the bush, or a little waterhole where the snakes, goannas and kangaroos came to drink.

All of the station activities centred on the mustering of wild scrub cattle, building fences and yards. I loved mustering and I would hang around the cattle yards, trying to help. Billy and I jumped on the back of a truck at every opportunity to go and kill a bullock for beef, or to check fences and bores.

In the very early days there were no cattle yards to hold the cattle, so everyone had to take it in turns to keep an eye on the herd to make sure they stayed where we wanted them to. Billy and I learnt to ride horses very early on and loved to do the night watch. This involved riding our horses slowly around the cattle at night to keep them settled so they did not wander too far away.

Everyone was allocated a two-hour watch, which they completed in pairs and then returned to camp to wake the next couple to take over. The first watch in the evening and the last watch at daylight were called the dogwatch. Everyone wanted either the first or the last watch so they could get a full night's sleep, but there was a pecking order, with the older and more experienced stockmen getting these shifts and the young ones getting the shifts at midnight and the early morning hours.

I always felt safe when I was out on watch. I was doing something I loved – riding a horse and being out in nature – and I also felt responsible, like I was contributing something. Even though I was a child, it was important to me that I played a part in the bigger enterprise that was Killarney. I never felt that I was separate from the adults, because we all had our jobs to do.

While the night-watchers were on horseback, everyone else slept with one ear to the ground. If there was the slightest change in the mood of the cattle everyone would sit bolt upright, ready to leap onto the back of a horse. If there were dingoes nearby, the cattle would be restless and were likely to take fright and rush.

The squawk of a night owl could be enough for the mob to lurch into a panic, stampeding blindly into the night. Both of these situations were to be avoided – not only could the cattle cause a lot of damage when they stampeded, they would also have to be mustered again, and that could take days.

When I was learning to ride, I was allowed to go on the first watch with either Banjo or Georgie while the rest of the camp were having dinner and settling for the night. Banjo would lead the way and I ambled along behind. He sang corroboree songs in a low monotone, over and over, for the whole of his shift. His soothing songs flowed across the thick dust into the sunset, willing the cattle to settle for the night.

I didn't realise then, but I was privileged to attend what were essentially private concerts every night. Banjo's songs were a part of my childhood – part of my Dreaming – and therefore precious to me. The Aboriginal stockmen also told us stories about debil debils and the Kadaitcha Man, just as Old Dora and Daisy did, although the stockmen's stories always seemed a little more scary. I was terrified of a story about the dingo that was bigger than a man, with eyes like car headlights, which would take you away in the middle of the night if you were naughty. The dingo could carry you in his teeth across the plains and up to the caves, high into the hills. I kept my manners and my eyes peeled in case I ever saw this dingo. I am happy to say that I must have been a good girl, because I never did see it.

At this age, Billy and I did everything together: getting into trouble, riding horses, fighting. We were often in competition with each other; if we were on horseback we'd be competitive about who was the best rider and how fast we could gallop, and we liked to show off our skills to the stockmen. As a girl, I felt I had to prove myself a little bit more. Not that anything was said to me – it was just a feeling I had, that I had to always keep up with the boys.

Within Aboriginal stockman society, women didn't really have much status. And while I wasn't brought up to believe that I was of lower status than my brothers – certainly not by my mother – I did feel quite competitive about wanting to be as good as the boys. And the expectations on me were that I should be good at everything, even though I was a girl and I was meant to be staying home and helping Mum. I wanted to do the same things that the blokes were doing, which was mustering and galloping around and learning to drive. But I didn't like changing tyres or killing snakes – I was happy to let the men do that!

Billy was very comfortable with his abilities and who he was. He was a good horseman, a good stockman, which meant he could do anything: he could fence, and fix motors. Being in the stockyards was how he grew up; it was part of his apprenticeship.

Mum wanted her girls to be treated the same way as her boys. She didn't stop me from driving, mustering and helping in the cattle yards with the drafting and branding.

Some of the things Billy and I got up to were outrageous. In retrospect, they were probably quite dangerous. No one would let their kids do those things now. But we learnt survival skills and hand—eye coordination, as well as an ability to move quickly, which stood us in good stead for sporting activities. These were life skills that would prove to be very useful for all of us. And we all survived our childhoods, so we must have been doing something right.

While Billy and I were getting up to mischief, Shing was still too young to join us; instead, she got on with being a cute little blonde-haired girl with flies in the corners of her eyes, dressed only in a pair of knickers, following the Aboriginal women around the camp. Everyone loved Shing.

7 Seasons in the Northern Territory

The cycle of life in the Northern Territory dictated everything: how we lived, how we worked. We couldn't hide inside a comfortable home – we didn't have one. We couldn't run away to a nearby town – Katherine was the closest and it was over 300 kilometres away.

The Northern Territory has only two seasons: the Wet and the Dry – according to white Australians, anyway. It is easy to see why this is so: the variance between the two is dynamic. In the Wet, one can expect torrential rain, flooding rivers, 40-degree heat in the shade and what seems like a million flies and mosquitoes.

In the Dry, the temperature can drop to minus overnight, the cold biting into your bones and sucking every bit of moisture out of your body; the blue skies are cloudless and the horizon endless.

Aboriginal people live by six seasons. They feel the subtle changes in the temperatures; they watch the receding water levels in the billabongs, take note of which animals are around to hunt and what berries, nuts and bush medicines are available. The seasons and the landscape are not only fundamental to the Aboriginal people and their spiritual stories, they are also fundamental to the day-to-day survival of people carving out a living in the bush.

For us there were the two distinct seasons out on the plains of the Victoria River Downs. Temperatures ranged from 50 degrees Celsius in the shade during the wet season and a million bush flies, to the dry season of bitterly cold winds that blew in off the Tanami Desert. Our hair would stand on end like straw and we'd have parched faces, cracked lips and two million flies all trying to live on us or in our food.

The period immediately before the wet season – always known as 'the build-up' – takes on a life of its own. The momentum gathers as the big white clouds roll in, cluttering up the once endless blue sky, with each day getting hotter, heavier and blacker. After a long dry season, the anticipation and expectation of rain built as we thrashed in our swags, sleepless, hot and sticky, and the mosquitoes bombarded our bare, damp skin. The build-up can turn the friendliest people into grumpy ones. When the bad-tempered cook started abusing everyone, we would smile and say, 'He's going troppo', or, 'He has mango madness'. That's what the seasons could do to us, and he was not the only one to behave that way.

All conversation revolved around rain: would it be late, would it be early, would it be a long wet season or a short one? Everyone had a theory about the Wet. A short, cold dry season meant a long wet season or vice versa; if it didn't rain before Christmas then we would get a cyclone in March.

As the clouds got bigger and raced across the sky, we waited, and waited, and bad tempers and bets increased. The seasons held us captive, if not hostage, and we had no choice but to live that way. We all understood that we were part of something so much bigger than any one individual or even our lively home: we might have our theories and our hopes about how the weather would behave, but it would always do whatever it wanted and we would obey.

In the dry season Killarney was brown and grey and khaki, with only the red dirt to provide some relief. In the wet season the creek would swell, the trees turned bright green, the grass grew emerald and the dirt became vermilion. It was so beautiful, and the land would heave with so much life, that we could almost forget that the dry season would come. But, inevitably, the ground would crack and the creek would become a trickle, and the cycle would continue again.

While the wet season was, to a certain degree, a time to take a break, there was also lots of work to be done, mainly repairing equipment and making new bridles, hobbles and ropes, pulling down bore pumps and vehicles and rebuilding them. The days were not so frantic in the Wet and we did get Sunday off.

On one occasion during the wet season we got bogged while returning from Victoria River Downs Station. We were stuck on a black soil plain with very few trees and spear grass standing well over our heads. Killarney was about 20 kilometres away, so Bill Tapp sent Banjo and Georgie to walk to the station and bring back a truck to pull us out.

As the hours passed and we got hungrier and hungrier, Old Dora decided that we would have to eat the grasshoppers that were whizzing around in plague proportions. Billy and I thought it was great fun as we laughed and pounced on the fat green and brown insects. I felt no remorse as they were thrown, alive, into the leaping flames and turned with sticks. We crunched on the crisp little bodies with relish. The grasshoppers didn't taste so good, but those poor little insects served their purpose by providing a bit of protein, a few vitamins, and filling a very hungry hole. Though I have had the pleasure of eating goanna, wild turkey, buffalo, wild bulls, lizards and a variety of birds, I have been grateful that grasshoppers are not a culinary delight I have had to eat again.

Bill Tapp chose not to eat the grasshoppers with us, but he waited patiently, periodically walking up to the truck and kicking a few tyres or wandering out to collect more logs and rocks to chock under the bogged vehicle.

It was never long before the wet season came to an abrupt end and we would be storing water in 44-gallon drums and drinking murky water from tanks, cattle troughs and muddy billabongs again. We still managed to break down regularly in the dry season as the old truck overheated.

All the roads in the bush were bad and caused much damage to vehicles, so that walking – or 'foot falcon', as we called it – was a common form of transport, as was getting about on horseback. Very few employees owned cars and most relied on the station for transport. It was not uncommon for people to walk from station to station during the wet season when there was plenty of water around, but you needed to have your wits about you and a means, such as a gun and matches, of catching and cooking some food along the way.

The dry season brought its own dangers, most importantly the drying dams, water shortages, and the much-feared bushfires in the later part of the year. Most often, the fires were ignited by a lightning strike in the build-up to the wet season.

Early on, a lot of the country was unfenced and fire control practices were unheard of. The first sign of a bushfire was a tendril of smoke that grew longer, wider and blacker on the horizon.

As the intensity of the dry season built, the grass dried and temperatures soared, we remained alert and kept a keen eye on the horizon for smoke. At the first sign, someone would jump in a vehicle and drive out to spot and identify the location and work out how many people and cars were required to fight it. There was no GPS technology back then.

While waiting for the spotter to get to the location and radio the information through, the station went into top gear, fuelling up Toyotas and the grader, loading and filling 44-gallon drums of water and hessian bags to fight the fires by hand. A convoy of vehicles would head out, with Bill Tapp giving orders over the two-way radio to go to different locations on the fire front. No one seemed to worry that kids were piled up on the back of the trucks, barefoot and wearing just shorts.

We would douse the hessian bags in water drums on the back of the ute and slap away at the flames while the grader roared along the front of the fire, mowing down flaming trees and leaping grass fires. We walked for miles, slapping at the flames way above our heads, at times racing back to a vehicle and speeding off just metres in front of the leaping flames that we could not contain. We'd return home with no eyebrows or eyelashes and burnt feet.

The snakes, goannas and kangaroos fled from the fire and the hawks and crows circled overhead. We stayed out all day and night, returning to the station or a nearby bore to refuel and fill the water drums. I always wanted to be right in the action, bashing a branch with green leaves against the fire snaking along the ground.

It was exciting for us kids to be fighting to save our country alongside the men. Some of the fires we fought were ferocious and destroyed hundreds of kilometres of country, raging and then smouldering for weeks on end.

As I got older, I decided that this was not really a great form of fun and I was not so keen to be jumping on the backs of vehicles to confront raging bushfires. How no one was killed, I will never know.

In later years, with better land-management practices, fences were built, fire breaks were cleared along the fence lines and the increasing cattle numbers meant the wild grasses were eaten down and there was less fuel for potential fires.

There are still fires but the pastoral industry now understands the environment better and practises controlled burnings at the right time of year, so that the burn intensity and damage to the flora and fauna are not as severe as they have been.

8 Hunting with Dora and Daisy

During the Dry, the old Aboriginal women often took us down the creek hunting. Daisy and Dora led the way across the black soil plain to the creek with a bundle of hunting tools. Dora would hobble along with her bundle of clothes slung across her shoulder and a long walking stick to prod into goanna and lizard holes. The stick was also good for probing into holes in tree trunks for wild honey known as 'sugar-bag' and looking for birds' eggs high up in their nests. Daisy sometimes carried a long stick with a burning coal on the end to start the fire for lunch; she would blow on the coal to keep it burning. But most of the time she started the fire by rubbing two sticks together over a little pile of dry, scrunched-up grass.

We went on our hunting trips well prepared, everyone loaded up with billycans, tea, sugar, flour, treacle and coarse salt. We took a piece of dry corned beef or raw rib bones covered in a greasy bit of rag, with ants crawling over it and complemented by a thick layer of black flies hanging around, just in case we couldn't find some other form of protein.

We'd race ahead of the old ladies, jumping from rock to rock, screeching and squealing in delight, looking for lizard eggs and goanna holes. Dora and Daisy followed, keeping a sharp eye on us.

Racing madly to the conkerberry tree, we'd eat the juicy red berries that turned our tongues purple. Then we'd skip over to the wild orange, which we called 'coolinyukka', its fruit the size of a golf ball with a soft red-orange centre, and bush bananas hanging from a vine. There was always a good supply of little dry berries called 'dog's balls' and the small wild onion known as 'brolga tucker'.

We would dig around the edge of billabongs for white ochre because the women needed it to paint themselves for their ceremonies. We'd squish the mud through our fingers below the water line, where we could feel the hard clumps in the mud. The white ochre would then be wrapped in a piece of old rag and used for corroborees. The yellow and orange sandstone rock ochre would be ground between two stones then bitten off in small chunks and broken down in the mouth with saliva, to make a smooth paste for body painting or decorating didgeridoos, boomerangs, nulla nullas and coolamons (a shovel-shaped carrying dish carved from the small trunk of the stinkwood tree, used to carry everything from firewood to food and babies).

Dora and Daisy made us our own special little coolamons and billycans to carry what we found. The adult billycans were made out of milk tins and our little ones were made out of jam tins. They made us steel digging sticks, shaped in the fire and pounded with a rock to give a flat, bladed end. I would dig away proudly, unearthing little piles of fresh wild potatoes, placing them on a coolamon to be cooked in the coals for lunch or taken home for the evening meal. They were yummiest, though, when they were raw.

Whenever we set off with Daisy and Dora it seemed like we walked hundreds of miles from home; later, when I was older, I looked at the area and realised it was only about three or four kilometres. It would just take us all morning to zigzag our way to the dinner camp under a tree in the dry riverbed.

The ancient paperbark trees and the winding creek bed were our playground. At home in familiar and safe surroundings we played barefoot, soles toughened like elephant skin, racing up and down the creek, climbing trees, mustering cattle on stick horses and waving stick guns. We were dirty and browned by the sun, bursting with excitement and energy, inquisitive about everything in our environment, around every corner, in every tree or under every rock. On each adventure there was sure to be a surprise – a goanna, snake or lizard, and, on the odd occasion, a scrub bull or thirsty cow to scare the living daylights out of us.

All the activity centred around the fire and the billycan of tea simmering on the hot coals. As the old women made johnnycakes and dug a hole to cook the wild yams, we kids would be clambering all around the riverbed, swinging out of trees, laughing and playing imaginary games. We never went too far, though, because Dora had warned us that there were devils and wild dingoes that carried little children away. She would call out along the riverbed, 'Don't go too far. That debil debil gonna get you!'

When lunch was ready we would settle in the shade with a pannikin of sweet black tea, which had its own special pungent taste, from the battered billycan; a billycan had to be leaking before it was replaced, as the tea never tasted as good in a shiny new tin. With bellies full of bush tucker, we would settle down in the midday heat to rest on a mattress of fresh gum leaves. I loved to snuggle against Daisy's belly; her dress smelled of goanna fat and fire overlaid with Sunlight soap.

In the stillness, the old ladies would tell us stories about the spirits. The women drew pictures of animals and spirits in the sand while telling their stories. They told us about the debil debils in the hills who took naughty children away from their families so they would never be seen again. The most terrifying stories were about the Kadaitcha Man, who roamed day and night across the country. The Kadaitcha Man was magical and knew who was breaking the law – that is those who disobeyed Aboriginal laws and their elders. He could come in the darkest of nights and remove your kidney fat with his bare hands, leaving no scars, and you would pine away, stop eating and die. It was a sad, lonely death – people knew that you had been 'sung' and you would be excommunicated from the family because of the curse.

These stories kept us in line, as they were designed to do. We would never have dreamt of being cheeky or answering back for fear of the spirits. The stories were endless: family, animals, spirits, and debil debils. There were songs about the stories and Daisy and Dora sang these as we settled down after lunch for a rest. The droning of the songs wrapped around the trees and travelled along the dry riverbed on wisps of the campfire smoke, sending us to sleep.

When the little ones slept, the women scratched through their hair for nits, crunching the live ones between their teeth or thumbnails. 'Ooohhhh, you got proper big ones,' they would laugh, placing the squirming nits into a tobacco tin to be counted when they were finished.

As the sun headed deep into the west, we would have one last play in the afternoon coolness before putting the fire out and covering it with dirt. The leftover food was carried in the coolamon or wrapped in a square piece of rag and hauled over our shoulders.

Everyone had something to carry, from the day's harvest of bush tucker to the billycan of sugar-bag, a tomahawk, or a nice, straight piece of tree branch ready to be carved into a fighting stick or coolamon. We would head off home, eyes peeled for the evening meal – hopefully a big, juicy goanna meandering its way into the creek for an evening drink.

If a goanna was sighted, the attack was like a scene out of an old cowboys-and-Indians movie, where we circled the animal, yelling and waving sticks. The sight and sound of Dora brandishing her big nulla nulla in the air, screaming at the top of her lungs – 'Git 'em that one, go dat way, come back 'ere' – was enough to give anyone a heart attack, let alone the poor unsuspecting goanna. We kids would all be jumping and squealing with excitement, adding to the cacophony of the kill, adrenaline pumping and hearts racing. Though both Daisy and Dora were big women, they moved with agility, easily clubbing the terrified creature to death.

As the goanna lay lifeless on the hot ground, Daisy would swoop in with glee, pick it up with one hand and haul it over her shoulder by the tail. Its crushed head and long, forked tongue dripped blood down the back of her dress, leaving a trail behind her. A black haze of bush flies and an exhausted group of kids followed the old women; we'd be filthy and hungry again, chattering about getting a big fire going for the feast of goanna and bush tucker.

As we passed our house on the way to the Aboriginal camp, we would ask Mum if we could go along to the camp to eat. She always allowed us to go and one of the camp people would walk us home in the dark after dinner.

These hunting trips occurred at least once a week. At all times we were prepared with our hunting equipment, so that we could leave when the old ladies called to us. The men never went hunting with the women and children; they went their separate ways, making boomerangs, didgeridoos and spears, and chasing bush turkeys and kangaroo for food.

9 Bush Tucker

Things that wouldn't have made sense to people who lived in houses and towns made perfect sense to us. It didn't occur to me that it was strange that instead of sleeping in the shed, we were sleeping beside it. It was more important, and logical, that the food was kept in the shed so it wouldn't get wet. It didn't matter so much if *we* got wet. We always had to think about the survival of Killarney; there was no point keeping the people dry if the flour was wet and couldn't be used to make damper.

Because there was no refrigeration in the early years, our diet was basic and repetitive – we couldn't have stored perishable fruit and vegetables, let alone anything more exotic like cheese, even if we could get hold of it. Instead there was plenty of tough beef to eat: fried, grilled, salted, stewed and roasted; and the stores consisted of tinned Sunshine milk, bags of sugar, cartons of loose tea leaves, flour, salt and baking powder, along with soap and tobacco.

Most vegetables came out of tins, and there were the occasional tins of salted butter, jam, peaches and apricots. There was no special cooking for kids – or anyone. We all ate the same thing, which was beef, and there were always lots of big stews, so I guess that was the soft food for the kids. All the little kids chewed on rib bones for their teething rings.

Most of the fresh beef was corned – that is, covered in coarse salt and laid out on an old wire bed frame to dry, the same process that these days produces beef jerky. This was our staple diet, interspersed with fresh steak and rib bones when we got a 'killer' – a steer that was to be killed for food – every week. The meat hung under the bough shed on wire hooks, covered in black flies, the blood dripping onto the ground. The fresh and corned beef were regularly supplemented by freshly killed bush turkey and goanna.

The beef was mostly accompanied by pumpkin, potato and onion – because they were the only vegetables that survived without refrigeration – followed by slabs of damper and tins of thick, bittersweet treacle for dessert. Curry powder was the only spice available and was mostly used to cover the taste of rotting beef that had green stuff growing around the edges. Everything was cooked in lashings of fat, salt and sugar.

All meals were eaten off enamel plates while sitting on the ground around the fire at night or under the trees during the day. The only table was a discarded wooden door placed on top of two empty 44-gallon drums. This table was used to prepare food, store the rations off the ground and discourage the ants. All the dry goods were kept in 4-gallon drums to keep the weather out, but they were not very useful at keeping the weevils and bugs at bay. The coarse salt and sugar came in plastic-lined hessian bags; they set like rock in the hot, humid weather and had to be broken and crushed into small pieces with a horse-shoeing hammer.

It wasn't all meat and veg, though – we ate plenty of bush tucker supplied by the Aboriginal people who also lived on Killarney: wild bananas and oranges, bush potatoes, paddy melons, sugar-bag and juicy red conkerberries. However, the harshness of that first year on Killarney affected us all. There was a severe shortage of food and we went for months without milk or vegetables and lived on sweet black tea and lots of fresh and salted beef.

When we went adventuring with Daisy and Doris, they'd often take us down to the creek. In one area there was a massive wild fig tree laden with plump brown fruit. We would gather these in billycans and if you ate too many you could find yourself spending a lot of time squatting behind a tree with a big bellyache. The gum trees oozed sticky clear gum that hardened into balls on the bark and we chewed on the rather bland white goo that looked and tasted like hardened glue. The bloodwood tree's crystallised red sap was kept in an old tobacco tin and mixed with hot water to use as dysentery medicine.

The favourite tucker for us sweet-toothed bush kids was sugar-bag, wild golden honey that we would find because of the little black bush bees hovering around a buzzing hole in a tree branch. We would climb the tree and scoop the honey out of the hole with a stick, twisting it around like a lollipop, filling the billycans and licking dripping honey from our hands. The wax from the sugar-bag was stored in milk tins to shape the mouthpieces of didgeridoos.

As the years went by and Killarney employed more people, Bill Tapp and Mum realised they needed to hire a cook. Mum never liked cooking much anyway and there was always too much that needed doing elsewhere.

Bush cooks are strange characters with wild reputations for being bad tempered. Cooking on a cattle station can be a thankless job: hot and tedious, with long days that begin before the sun rises and finish long after it sets.

We were blessed the day Old Micko entered our lives. Our stomachs knew he was one of the best things to happen to us! Micko was a little man, thin and wiry, about five foot one; he had been a sapper in the 6th Division of the Australian Army that fought in the Owen Stanley Range in Papua New Guinea as well as in the Middle East. Micko had the tips of his fingers missing on one hand. Whenever I asked what had happened to his fingers he would answer, 'I kept the grenade and threw the pin away.'

Micko's entire wardrobe consisted of white Bonds singlets, khaki short shorts and a little towelling tennis hat to cover his balding head. His shoe wardrobe was a range of different-sized rubber thongs.

Micko was a placid, kind-hearted man who was also the most amazing cook and gardener. He set up a large half-acre vegetable garden with rows of elegant nodding sunflowers around the perimeter. We ate thick yellow corn on the cob and bright orange carrots, fresh tomatoes, juicy green beans and bowls of fresh peas. He grew so much produce that we gave away boxes of excess vegetables to the stock inspectors, pilots and truckies.

Micko filled large coffee jars with pickled beetroots, chillies and chutneys, and took care of more than a hundred chooks, feeding them the garden and kitchen scraps, and collecting the eggs. All this, as well as feeding up to forty people three big meals and two smokos a day.

When he first arrived, in 1969, he achieved all of this out of an incredibly hot kitchen with a huge wood-fired stove, until a new brick kitchen with air conditioning and big stainless-steel gas stoves was built. Micko helped with the design of the new kitchen in 1970 and it was his pride and joy to have one of the most modern station kitchens in the Northern Territory, with large stoves and sinks big enough to swim in.

He made sixteen double loaves of fresh fluffy bread with golden crusts every day, getting up at four in the morning to start the dough. He cooked massive trays of crispy baked potatoes, pumpkin and onion to accompany big slabs of roast beef with jugs of steaming homemade gravy. Big pots boiled endlessly on the top of the stove, filled with corned beef and large yellow flaps of fat rendering down into dripping.

When Micko cooked for Christmas, we ate like royalty. He prepared every morsel of food lovingly and with pride. He shook off compliments with the air of one who knew there was no better than him. Christmas sent Micko into rapture, because he had access to a wide range of special ingredients, including an extra supply of vanilla essence, whisky, port and sherry for the puddings and cakes. He always ordered double amounts of vanilla essence, which had alcohol in it, to ensure there was a cup for the pudding and a cup for the creator.

The kitchen would be a production line of fruitcakes, mince pies, coconut ice, peanut brittle, chocolate fudge, marshmallows and homemade sauces and gravies. We loved it, as he would let us lick the bowls clean and test the goodies. The ham was wrapped and cured in the cold room and large headless turkeys lined up all white and prickly waiting for their turn in the oven.

Cherries, plums, apricots, peaches and pears all looked too good to eat. The Aboriginal children eyed the fruits suspiciously and were often too frightened to taste them as they had never seen them before.

Micko was a master of making mouth-watering meals out of nothing. A few egg whites and sugar beaten for half an hour produced beautiful meringues; sugar and water made tooth-cracking toffees. An old slab of beef rubbed with a few dried herbs, Worcestershire sauce and cooked with vegies in the camp oven brimming with fat became a tasty, belly-filling meal.

With Christmas over, still in the midst of the wet season, our diet would revert to stringy dried bits of corned beef, pumpkin, potatoes and onions for breakfast, lunch and dinner; baked, stewed and boiled, anything for a little variety in presentation of the same monotonous ingredients. The bread was made out of stale weevilly flour and when the yeast ran out, crusty dampers were baked in the camp ovens. The delicious flavours of Christmas would become a distant memory and we'd count down the days until new supplies would arrive.

10 Kids' Games

My first best friend was Old Dora's daughter Nita. She was the youngest of the ten children in her family and I was destined to be the eldest of ten in my family.

Nita was tall for her age and thin, with a head of thick, curly black hair. The three middle fingers on her left hand were missing so the hand looked like a claw with just a thumb and little finger. This was a birth defect that didn't have any adverse effect on her ability to climb trees, make fire, dig for bush potatoes and kill goannas, just as all Aboriginal girls did every day.

We spent most of our time going hunting with Dora, whom we both called Mum. Nita was a couple of years older than me and was approaching puberty, and it would soon be time for her to be handed over to her promised husband – this happened to Aboriginal girls once they developed breasts and had their first period. The timing, therefore, wasn't fixed, but Nita and I both knew it was coming. Dora guarded Nita jealously from the young men in the camp and she would give them a screaming tongue lashing at the slightest sideways glance. She didn't want Nita's attention going anywhere else, nor did she want any other man making a play for her daughter before Nita came of age.

One day, Old Dora heard that one of the older white men on the station was interested in Nita. She flew into a fury, screaming abuse from the camp about a kilometre away, limping and swinging a nulla nulla above her head. Between the yelling she would sing a type of chorus, a curse on the man. Every so often she would stop and pull off a dress and fling it onto the ground behind her, then start up the abuse again. She did this about four times, each time revealing another dress, until she came to a standstill at the front of the mechanics' workshop in her red floral petticoat. She stood there, gleaming with sweat as she continued to curse him. Everyone on the station heard and watched in awe and terror of the little dynamo, limping along on her bag foot. She left no doubt in anyone's mind that her daughter was off limits.

The mechanic hid behind the shed till the dust settled and kept well out of Nita and Dora's way from then on.

All of Dora's older daughters had been married off to their promised husbands. They lived on neighbouring cattle stations and had large extended families, as there were two or three wives to each husband. Nita was Dora's baby and she didn't want to lose her before it was absolutely necessary. Yet it was also important to the family honour and skin system that Nita go to the man she had been promised to before she was born.

Nita, Billy and I played together all the time. We didn't have any formal schooling in the early days so we had plenty of time to get into mischief and make up games that suited both our cultures. We spent all our time running away from the debil debils while being attacked by (imaginary) cowboys and Indians. We fought them with stick guns and galloped off on stick horses and lay flat on the ground behind a rock, and had shoot-outs with the baddies hiding behind trees and down gullies.

We made shanghais: a forked piece of tree branch that had two slings made from rubber bands cut from old tyre tubes tied to the forks, and a small leather piece to hold a stone to shoot galahs that gathered at the water trough, so we could cook them on a fire.

Nita taught us how to make fire by rubbing sticks together and we would roast birds and lizards for our dinner. We collected empty tobacco tins, crushed one edge of the tin in, made a hole in each side and tied the tins to our feet to make horse tracks. We had races, rolling on empty fuel drums across the dirt to see who could get the farthest without falling off. We would run on the rolling drum, the rocky ground sending it in different directions, our arms flailing for balance. The drum would gather speed and eventually we would fall heavily onto the hard, hot ground. It was a game that left us with many bruises and twisted ankles, but this did not deter us from the thrill of the competition.

We were always up to something. One day Billy and Nita were playing with a box of matches and burnt down the old wooden saddle shed with a tin roof and a wind break wall made of dried branches. Everyone was yelling and running towards the fire with buckets of water to put it out.

Billy and Nita fled down to the creek to hide for a while, because they thought they would get into trouble, but the situation settled down and the shed was rebuilt without too much upset.

Another time, Nita, Billy and I were returning from one of our many trips to the creek chasing goannas, looking for sugar-bag and playing games. We had to climb through a barbed-wire fence. Nita was agile and fast and usually led the way. She bounded up over the barbed-wire fence, slipped and fell, catching her leg on the wire. She swung upside down on the fence with the ragged point of the steel picket stuck into the back of her bent knee. Billy and I leveraged her off the picket to reveal a large, flapping wound. Blood spurted everywhere.

We didn't have anything to tie around the wound to stop the flow so we just slung one arm each over our shoulders and dragged Nita along the ground, all three of us bawling our eyes out. Sobbing for breath, we stopped under a tree to rest. Nita was crying in pain, and Billy and I were crying in terror at the blood pouring from her leg and the fear of getting into trouble for being so stupid and going down to the creek without adults.

When we arrived home, Old Dora started screaming in fright and gave us all a good tongue lashing while wrapping a long piece of dirty rag around Nita's wound. When everyone settled down we then went to see Mum, who cleaned the wound with Dettol and bandaged it up with some antiseptic ointment and a clean white cotton bandage.

Nita was incapacitated for a few days afterwards and limped around with a little homemade walking stick, but it wasn't long before she was mobile again and we were looking for a new adventure.

We loved playing down the creek. In the dry season we climbed the trees and ran up and down the riverbed, creating tracks and camps. Every afternoon in the wet season we walked to our favourite swimming spot, where we had made a large mud slide into the water on one bank, while on the other we created a firing range with a pile of rounded mud balls for fights.

The old women sat up on the sand bank with a fire and billycan of tea simmering, cooking bush tucker and making little johnnycakes for lunch. They settled fights and arguments and periodically lunged into the water to save one of the smaller kids from drowning, growling at us for not being careful and looking after them.

We had very busy lives entertaining ourselves. We would spend days playing make-believe in the old cars at the dump, making car noises, crunching gears and doing skids around imaginary corners. We dressed imaginary wounds and broken legs and drove furiously to town to save someone's life. We would muster cattle into the yards, brand them and load them onto the trucks to take them to town to the meatworks, and go shopping to pick up the stores. We made old milk tins into stilts by piercing a hole in each side and attaching a long wire handle to lift the tins in unison with our feet. We made up songs and chattered constantly in pidgin English.

We made a whole village out of old bits of tin and fencing wire tied to the side of a car or a tree, and little paths and tracks between the houses. We found old wooden boxes and lined them with empty food packets and tins in the kitchen. We used hubcaps for a washing-up dish and jam tins for cups.

Nita, Billy and I each had our own house and we made a little bush broom to rake and clean the dirt around the outside to define the front garden. We would take some beef and bread and a little billycan of water from home up to the playground. There we made a fire and invited each other to share meals and a pannikin of tea while we talked about how to build important things such as cattle yards and fences, and how to muster cattle.

We loved to go on the annual trip with the stockmen to cut new branches for the bough sheds. This ritual happened after the wet season to re-roof the bough sheds and the humpies that the Aboriginal people lived in. One person would drive very slowly while others chopped the new fleshy branches from the young trees with an axe and throw them onto the back of the truck.

We would run alongside helping, but the best part was when the truck was piled up to the roof and we would climb into the beautiful-smelling eucalypt branches and hide from each other.

On one of these trips, one of the Aboriginal men had chased down a big goanna and concussed it with a blow to the back of its head with the axe. The apparently lifeless goanna was thrown onto the truck. We sat huddled under the branches beside the bloodied lizard, giggling and salivating about what a juicy feed Mr Goanna was going to be that night, when all of a sudden he came alive.

Scratching and frenzied, he ran over the top of me and flew off the back of the moving truck onto the ground.

We scrambled and screamed and banged on the roof of the truck. It came to a screeching halt and we all fell out – in terror, in my case. The others took after the goanna to retrieve him for dinner, but he was too fast this time, despite the almost fatal knock to the head, and disappeared into the bush. We were hysterical with fright and laughter. The only proof that we hadn't imagined the whole thing was the small pool of blood that remained in the back of the truck.

11 Where's the Water?

The search for water was a never-ending struggle as Killarney was a dry block with no permanent waterholes. The Coolibah and Battle creeks raged into the massive Victoria River system in the wet season and lay dusty and dry for months in the dry. The Mayvale Bore was only ten kilometres off the Buchanan Highway but produced a meagre 150 gallons of water per hour. The Mayvale water was also limey and rank; it was barely enough to quench the thirst of the family, stockmen and horses, let alone a mob of thirsty cattle.

When Bill Tapp first moved to Killarney the most urgent need was to find a stable water supply. He always seemed to be working frantically, building houses, building new fences, putting in water bores and building turkeys' nests, which were mud waterholes created by pushing the dirt into mounds with a bulldozer to form a large above-ground dam.

Despite the difficulties, we lived happily for the first two years at Mayvale Bore, even though the water supply was thick, dark and murky, and the quality and quantity dropped to unsustainable levels. Soon, everyone suffered from constant dysentery. Given that we couldn't survive without water, it was time to move and for Bill Tapp to find a place to build a permanent homestead.

Bill Tapp decided that we must move a further 30 kilometres off the main road and into the centre of the property, to Gallagher's Bore, where the water quality and supply were better. It was also a more central location to work from and less barren than Mayvale Bore.

He hired bore drillers from Alice Springs, 1500 kilometres south, to search for a better water supply for the station and set up a number of bores and troughs. We observed the men practising the ancient methods of water divining, which involved making a T-shaped wand out of fencing wire and walking around with it pointed to the ground.

When the wire detected a water table, it would quiver and pull towards the water and the drillers would set up in that area. Still, they spent a long time drilling and had a lot of trouble finding enough drinkable water in some areas.

With Killarney being 2819 square kilometres in area, we needed quite a few water bores spread strategically across the station so that cattle could be moved back to the central area for branding and trucking off to the meatworks. Having good bores made it easier to muster the cattle, who had to come to the bore every day to drink.

In 1963 we packed up our 'home'. Everything fitted on the back of a truck and was moved to the new location to await the construction of our new house. None of us was going to miss the bough shed – it might have been our shelter but in reality the whole of Killarney was our home. Which was just as well, because we would live in a new bough shed while the homestead was being built. It didn't make much difference to me – it had been great fun sleeping in our swags, then we'd had the verandah of the shed, and now there was a new shed.

The only existing resident at Gallagher's Bore was a little old white man called Bill Ardill, who was about seventy years old and had originally come from New South Wales. He was so grimy and dirty that his skin was brown and his white beard was stained yellow from tobacco. Bill lived in a broken-down shack that looked as if it would topple over at any minute. The shack was dark and hot, and we never went inside.

Old Bill had a large outdoor fire where he cooked his food and made large slabs of thick soap, and a big wooden table with a set of large butcher knives. He had eight ferocious blue heelers that followed him everywhere – another reason for us to stay away!

Every morning Old Bill ingested half a grain of strychnine – granules of dingo poison, similar to rat poison – as an all-round medicine and vitamin pill. This was called a 'heart starter' and it was common practice among the old drovers and bushmen to self-medicate with this poison. Old Bill swore by the remedy. It must have worked for him, because he was incredibly healthy and strong.

Other common bush remedies included oil of cloves for toothache – this was a prized medicine – Bex powders, and rum, which was thought to remedy pretty much everything else. Old Bill also liked to boil up pots of green pig weed, which was apparently some sort of wild vegetable containing essential vitamins. He was very fit and alert, so we assumed that he knew what he was doing.

Old Bill spent all his time checking the water level on two bores and keeping the pumps going. He walked around the only paddock near the bore, twelve square miles, every morning with his dogs. He was a well-spoken gentleman who had read widely and seemed to know everything about everything, particularly about plants and bush food.

He kept almost entirely to himself and rarely interacted with the stockmen or Aboriginal people, although he visited my mother, who lived in her shed just 100 metres away, once a week to share a cup of tea and talk about world politics.

Everything revolved around water in those first few years. Our first home was only a few hundred metres away from the bore. The shed had fibro walls, a kitchen, an old wood stove and 44-gallon drums full of water outside the back door. There was an outside bathroom that consisted of a shower, made from a tin bucket with holes in the bottom slung over a beam, three walls and no door, on a slab of cement. The wind whipped through the shower in the cold weather so we didn't use it too often. The kids got bathed in a bucket of warm water.

The old rusty brown shed became the men's kitchen when we moved into the fibro house. We had a new 'long drop' toilet with three walls built for our private family use, about 100 metres from the fibro house, and this one had a roof and a door that didn't close. Many a time we had encounters with king brown snakes, scorpions and great big redback spiders in that toilet. It was the scariest place on the station and a quick squat behind the wood heap – also home to snakes, spiders and lizards – was a much more attractive option.

12 Family Life

Having Mum's brothers Boko and Uncle Jimmy around made Killarney seem like it wasn't so different to Nana's house in Katherine – it was just a bigger, more rugged version with no walls and no windows. We also had the family from the camp – not just our uncles but the other stockmen – as well as the Aboriginal families who lived with us.

Everyone lived the same way, under the same conditions, and everyone had a role to play in the running of the camp. The kids got to be kids for a while, but not forever – there would be jobs for us too. In the meantime, we could run wild and have fun; we could learn about the land and what it could provide us with; we'd live through the seasons and learn how they affected everyone. I just lived each day as it came.

This was not the case for Bill Tapp, who was always planning more paddocks to control the cattle, more access into the scrub country, more water bores and income to pay for the stores, vehicle and repairs. For the rest of us, we didn't think about the next day. We couldn't – we didn't know what the next day would bring. It was a way of life that kept things simple. It was a way of life that, as a small child, I learnt to love.

Mum's fifth child, Joe, was born in December 1963; the sixth, Ben, in June 1965 and he was followed by William in July 1966 – that made a run of four boys in the middle of the family. I never felt pressured to help out with the babies each time a new one arrived, it was just part of life. I looked after the little ones around me, the ones who had grown out of babyhood, although I ended up doing a lot of bathing, changing nappies and making bottles anyway. I felt like I was doing my share.

I revelled in family life. I loved the way we lived and all those kids being around, and even when they got a bit older and were a nuisance, I loved them anyway. They were always there. Just part of life, like having a new pile of poddy calves to feed. There were lots of nappies and baby bottles around the house for so many years that for me it was normal.

Our lives as kids weren't that much different to those of the adults around us. We were living in a very close community – it was only a couple of hundred metres from our shed to the men's quarters and a couple of hundred metres more to the stockyards. Everything was so close that people could watch out for us.

All the kids, black and white, were just part of life on the station. We weren't excluded from anything, including the hard things. We didn't have a flash house where kids were sent off to the bedroom when the sun went down because adults wanted to talk. Certainly, the first ten years of life on Killarney was not like that at all. It was all in together, all the time, for every single person who worked there.

There were times when the Aboriginal people would receive messages of the death of a family member somewhere in the district. These messages were often delivered through dreams or spirits, or sometimes a member of the family had walked across the country to deliver the news.

All the camp would go into full mourning. Dora and Daisy would wail long and loud, swaying bare-breasted in their half-slips, hitting themselves on the head with a rock until blood ran down their faces. The men sang long into the night in time to clap sticks and the haunting sound of the didgeridoo. The men and women did not mix during these times and the men carried out their ceremonies and mourning in an area at least half a mile away from the women.

They sang of their sorrow and asked the spirits to take the dead person back to their country, to their creation. They would dance and drag leaves along behind them to clear away the tracks of the dead person so that the bad spirits could not find them. The rest of the station people paid their respects by keeping their distance and allowing the mourners to return to work when they were ready.

This mourning and sadness would go on for days and days, and once it was over no one spoke that person's name again. Sometimes people would say that they saw that person in their dreams or that the spirit had come back as a dingo or bush turkey, a goanna or a snake. I always accepted that this was real – it didn't seem strange. It was what I'd grown up with, after all.

•

Life might have been hard at times but Mum always managed to make it fun in the simplest way. She made sure everyone on the station had a birthday cake and she bought new clothes, powders and perfumes for the women and children, including her own, through mail-order catalogues. We had dress-up parties on the front verandah and everyone dressed as a cowboy, an Indian or a Mexican.

There were no fairy or Cinderella dresses in our dress-up box and our outfits were easily converted from everyday wardrobes with the addition of a coloured blanket thrown over shoulders, a black moustache drawn on with a pen, or a hessian bag cut up for an Indian suit and some cockatoo feathers tied into a hat band.

Captain Victor Pedersen, the Salvation Army minister who flew a tiny Tiger Moth plane that looked like it was held together by sheets of paper and calico, often brought films when he visited the station. He'd set up and project the film onto the back wall of our house. We would sit on blankets on the ground with the whole community – the Aboriginal people, the cook, the bore runner, the mechanic and the stockmen – to watch scratchy black and white reel-to-reel movies that regularly had an insect bustling around behind the lens. The projector often overheated and at the crucial moment the film would begin to burn around the edges and melt as we watched it all happening on the wall. We would all groan with disappointment and wait patiently until he made repairs, which meant the story jumped from the middle of a scene to a completely different one because the damaged piece of film had been cut out and the remainder stuck back together with clear sticky tape. This was the outback version of watching TV with our family.

13 Animal Antics

Bill Tapp's obsessive and kind nature became clear to me quite early on. He checked and double-checked that gates were closed and pumps and power points were turned off. He loathed cruelty to animals. Bill Tapp would not allow us to kill or hurt anything and this included insects, ants and flies. When the toilet clogged up with frogs he would make us take them down to the creek in a bucket to find a new home. Mum said that she knew the frogs all returned happily to the toilet the next day!

On one occasion, Sammy the pet donkey got into the kitchen and ate all the loaves of freshly baked bread sitting on the bench, knocking over drums of flour, billycans of tea and bags of sugar. All that day's food was a big mishmash mess on the stone floor. Mum was so furious.

She chased him up the flat with a bush broom. But in the end she just had to clean it up and start all over again.

If a bird was hit while we were out driving, Bill Tapp would lean out of the car window and yell, 'Did any of you kids see that bird hit the bonnet? Do you think it died straightaway?' When this happened at night, we would snuggle down under the blankets in the back of the vehicle and pretend we were all fast asleep.

'Did any of you kids see that bird hit the bonnet? Do you think it died straightaway?' he would yell louder.

We would all reply, 'Yesssss, it's dead!'

But Bill Tapp would stop and methodically inspect the front grille of the car to see if the bird was wedged in there and possibly still alive. If there was no dead bird in the grille, he would set off. Ten minutes down the road he would ask again.

'Are you sure that you saw that bird? Was it killed properly?'

'Yessss,' our little voices shrilled through the darkness in our most convincing fashion, all the while trying to act very exhausted and tired and burrowing deeper into the swag. But we knew what was coming.

'All right, you kids keep a lookout on both sides and let me know if you see the bird.' He'd turn the vehicle around and head back the way we came.

All the little kids would lean over the sides of the Toyota, cold wind whipping around, looking for the remains of a wounded or dead bird.

'Do you think it was about here?' Bill Tapp would ask while we searched in vain for some bird feathers.

'Yesssss . . . it's dead,' we would call back, trying to get it over and done with as none of us had taken any notice and just wanted to get into town.

'I think I'll just go a bit further, I think it was nearer to the Delamere turn-off, and if it's not there then it must be all right.'

We would continue to creep along the road, little heads peering out into the dark, looking for a dead bird. If Bill Tapp spotted feathers on the road, we would have to get off the back of the vehicle and search for a corpse.

There was me, the eldest, aged about nine and my younger brothers and sister aged down to about four years. We were all terrified of the dark and would scrabble around to see if there was an injured bird anywhere close by; however, we rarely found the creature and were relieved to be able to crawl onto the back of the vehicle and curl up under the blankets to resume our trip when Bill Tapp would finally turn the vehicle in the right direction, after much coaxing from Mum in the front seat.

My mother later told me he would continually ask her for clarification and reassurance. Did she see the bird? Should he turn back? Did she think it died instantly?

No one was allowed to kill any animals for any reason other than if they were suffering or for food. We killed at least one beast a week for the meat supply. Despite the fact that the stockman, usually the head stockman, Sandy Shaw, had been doing this for years, he would still get a half-hour lecture about how to kill the animal humanely – Bill Tapp knew that animals had to die for us to be fed, but he also thought there was a right way to kill them.

'Make sure the cattle are settled,' he'd say. 'When you have picked out the killer, make sure it's right under the tree and that you have the gun ready and steady. Make a noise so when it looks up, you can shoot it in the middle of the forehead.'

These instructions were given every single time, month after month, year after year. We kids went to most of the kills and though it sounds harsh, it was a weekly outing for us, and we would always be questioned by Bill Tapp when we got home.

'Did Sandy kill that bullock with one shot?'

'Of course.' We would all nod our heads vigorously. 'Yes, he killed it with one good shot, right in the middle of the forehead.' Which, of course, he did!

Bill Tapp loved his animals and though he was very much a pacifist, someone who didn't like violence, I once saw him punch a stockman for hitting a horse over the head with a hammer. The stockman was swearing and jerking the horse around because it would not stand still to have its shoes fitted. Bill Tapp said to the man, 'How would you like someone hitting *you* over the head every time you moved?'

The cattle, all 30 000 head of them, were treated with care and compassion. When mustering, Bill Tapp would make sure that all cows with new calves were left behind in the paddock so they were not rushed or trampled in the mob. He said we could get them next time around when they were older and stronger – he didn't want to stress the mothers or brand the calves when they were too little.

One of the favourite family stories that developed into the folklore surrounding Bill Tapp was about him stopping a mob of a thousand head of cattle and not letting them through a gate because there was a big track of ants furiously marching across the road. He placed some bread and syrup on the ground to make a track to divert the ants while the stockmen and the cattle waited patiently for him to signal that they could continue.

Most afternoons, Bill Tapp would go for a drive to check the stud horses and cattle in the paddocks close to home. As he drove he would question Mum.

'Did the chestnut mare look lame?'

'No, I don't think so,' she would reply.

'Are you sure she didn't have a bit of limp on the onside front foot?'

'No, I didn't notice.'

He would then lean out the window and ask us kids the same question.

'Noooo, she didn't look lame to me.'

We knew what was coming next.

'Oh well, I'll just go back and check.'

He would turn the vehicle around and go back to double-check, making the horse trot by, while having a deep discussion with Mum about whether the mare had a slight limp or not. If he could not be convinced, which was more often than not, he would write down the horse's brand number and description, and send someone out on horseback to recheck the next day, and then the questions would start again: 'Did you get up close to have a look at that mare? Did you make her trot? Did she have any cuts on that leg? Do you think her foal is getting enough milk?'

One of the many times that the bore broke down, we had to move some cattle closer to water. When the cattle got a smell of the water at our house, they would come charging, frantically trying to get to the water in the drums.

At some stage, a big bull got into the shower and he didn't know how to get out. It was dark and there were cows outside, knocking over our precious drums, looking for water. Mum had to get the stock whip out to try to get rid of the bull. She had no idea how to crack it, but thought it might help if she swung it around her head and yelled. The bull was bellowing and blowing saliva and snot everywhere. The kids were all piled in the corner of the bedroom – which also had no door – wide-eyed with fear. It seemed to take forever, but the bull eventually found his way out.

14 Killarney Grows Bigger and Bigger

Bill Tapp researched and planned everything to do with Killarney meticulously, from the buildings to the breed of cattle and the type of vehicle he would purchase. And he had planned this move to Gallagher's Bore with the same attention to detail.

His first job at the new station site was to build a large set of cattle yards. All the posts were hand cut, with the lancewood rails being transported from the Murranji Stock Route, approximately 80 kilometres away.

After Sam was born, Bill Tapp converted a shed 'up the flat' at Gallagher's, now called Killarney, for the family to move into, as Mum was pregnant again. This initial shed was a large room with a rusty brown corrugated-iron roof and four corrugated-iron walls, no door and dirt floors.

We lived there for a short time, less than a year, but at last we now had some shelter from the rain and wind. The shed had a lumpy mattress on a board with four five-gallon drums for legs, and that's what Mum and Bill Tapp slept on. There was a baby's cot and the rest of us slept on the floor in swags.

The men camped outside in their swags in the dry season. There was a table and a couple of rusted metal chairs and stacked boxes for shelving and storing clothing. The toilet about 150 metres away was a long drop, a hole dug in the ground with a cut-off 44-gallon drum over it. The drum had a hole cut in the top. It was surrounded by three tin walls and no roof, facing out into the bush. It was so hot you could not sit on the drum, so it had two wooden planks to crouch on. The smell was indescribably bad and the black haze of flies could be seen from miles away. The shed was quite close, only about 50 metres away from the mechanics' workshop where all the men camped; however, Bill Tapp was in full swing with setting up his dream home now that he had identified the permanent position for the station. Nothing would stay the same for long.

In the late 1960s the men built a large corrugated-iron workshop shed with a wood stove in a corner, and the single men lived there, camping outside on wire bed frames in the dry season and moving into the shed in the wet season. The shed was also used as a workshop to fix vehicles, for storage and as the station store. Generally, people got on pretty well – they were adept at living together, making allowances for a wide range of idiosyncrasies and cultural differences. A significant portion of the workers lived in the Aboriginal camp a kilometre away from our shed; the camp was always visible from our home because Killarney was so flat.

In the early days Mum operated a small store in a cramped, hot room at the end of the mechanical workshop, offering the most basic of essentials: matches and tinned tobacco, powdered milk, tea, flour, needles and cotton, sugar, salt, blankets, soap, razor blades, treacle, jam, tinned peas and golden syrup.

The store was replenished every few months, depending on the weather and who was travelling into or out of Katherine to pick up the goods. A big order had to be done in November to get us through the wet season because the roads were usually impassable until about May the following year.

This order would include all the tinned food, tea, sugar, salt, and flour as well as rolls of fencing wire, steel, fencing pickets, pliers, nuts and bolts, tin, cement, and rolls of leather to repair saddles and make new bridles and halters.

The goods were ordered over the crackly two-way radio, or by a handwritten order if someone was going to town. Everything was bought from the only two stores in town, Cox's Store and Katherine Stores. Sometimes Mum would order in fancy things such as hair oil, powder, hair pins, scented soaps, and pieces of cheap, colourful cotton fabric, needles and cotton for the Aboriginal women to sew clothes.

Mum would open the station store for an hour or so once a week and the workers would line up to get their supplies. She would write their purchases in a book and deduct them from the wages that she wrote up in the blue leather-bound wages book at the end of each month. I loved helping Mum and looking at all the new shiny packets and tins of food lined up neatly on the shelves.

As we lived in the corrugated-iron shed, Bill Tapp began to build onto another tin shed further away. It had three tiny rooms with no doors, little playhouse windows with tin louvres, a tin roof and a rammed-earth floor. Bill Tapp added fibro walls and another two rooms, a verandah and a cement slab floor. The food, saddles and pretty much everything else were stored in the rooms so they wouldn't get wet.

We all slept in one area, where the rain often swept in and soaked everyone and everything. There was no running water. In the wet season the water leaked through the nail holes in the roof and in the dry season the bitter winds and dust swirled through the creaking walls.

Water was carted from the bore on the back of a truck in used 44-gallon drums and deposited near the kitchen wall. When it was needed for cooking, washing and having baths, the water was siphoned into buckets. There was a gutter on the shed roof that spilled water into some open-top drums in the wet season.

While more fences were being built, our new and final house was built in 1969 with grey cement bricks handmade on site. The bricks were a mix of grey cement powder and sand carted from the creek and pressed firmly into a metal mould that made six bricks at a time. We had a lot of fun making the bricks and seeing our new home grow.

Bill Tapp had drawn a design by hand and given it to the builder. The low-set house had a large kitchen and lounge room area. There was a big bedroom with an ensuite for Mum and Bill Tapp, and an adjoining small room with no door for the baby. There was a pantry/storeroom and this was also where the medicines were kept. There was a massive big room divided by a built-in wardrobe, with two sets of double bunks in the main area for the boys and Shing and me. Out the back door from our room was a separate building about 50 metres away with an office, outside toilet, laundry and storeroom. The whole of the front of the building was covered by a large, sweeping verandah.

A school was built with one large classroom and a single bedroom and kitchenette for the teacher.

As soon as the brick house was habitable we moved from the fibro and tin shed into it, even though it didn't have doors or windows. Our old shed was then used as the men's kitchen and sleeping quarters. One room was set aside for the cook to sleep in, the middle room was a pantry, and the third room was for the head stockman to sleep in. All the other employees camped along the back verandah with their swags laid out on wire beds.

The front verandah was set up as the dining room, open to the bitter winds of the dry season and whipping rain in the wet season. This served as the men's quarters until an eight-bedroom men's quarters was built in the early 1970s along with two 'married houses' – two-bedroom cottages for the white married employees such as a mechanic and head stockman.

These were followed with a new 'men's kitchen', which was a large dining room on one end and a state-of-the-art kitchen with stainless-steel sinks, big gas ovens and industrial fridges in the middle, and a guest dining room on the other end.

Finally two single-bedroom motel units were built for the ever-growing number of visitors. There wasn't too much spare room in our house for extras.

In the early 1970s Bill Tapp decided to pull down the old wooden cattle yards he had built by hand and make new steel yards. He wanted them to be the biggest and the best in the country.

Mum and Bill Tapp planned the layout of the station, including gardens, deciding to plant hundreds of *Ficus hilli* trees in straight rows along driveways and house fences, providing much-needed shade around the buildings and cattle yards. The trees spread octopus-like tentacles of roots that lifted cement floors and cracked walls in their burrowing to find water in the hard, black soil.

Mum did not like cooking and could not sew, but she loved gardening and planted trees and flowers everywhere. She loved petunias and had them along the front of the house and school and in garden beds at the 'Recreation' area. The little coloured flowers flourished in planters made out of cut-off fuel drums and old tyres.

There was a succession of gardeners who liked their alcohol too much, who mowed and weeded and invariably pulled out the new petunia seedlings or mowed over new shrubs just taking hold. Despite this, the bougainvilleas exploded in their glorious reds, mauves and purples over gateways, fences and tank stands. The poinciana trees along the front of the men's dining room bloomed in a canopy of red fire in September.

As more and more people came to Killarney, Bill Tapp's empire grew – and he had more and more responsibility. He had to make sure that everyone was looked after, if not luxuriously then adequately. All up there were about twenty-five people working on Killarney when I was young, although we started with just ten. This increased to about forty people in the early 1970s. New people were coming into our lives, people with the skills needed to build a cattle station from the ground up. Fencers and yard builders, bore drillers and people to fix and maintain the bores, saddlers to repair saddles and cooks to feed the growing population, most of them staying for ten or twenty years. As the cattle numbers grew we needed more paddocks and more stockmen, and we needed more expertise. More fences were built to contain the cattle and more houses built to accommodate the people.

15 Monsters from the Deep and Other Stories

Old Norman Jensen was one of the many characters who spent time on Killarney. He lived in various locations around the station as he searched and drilled for the elusive underground water. He, like everyone at the time, lived frugally and in incredibly rough conditions, just a tarpaulin stretched between trees to shade his food and belongings. He camped out under the stars in his swag in the Dry and under a makeshift lean-to in the Wet.

In 1965, Norm was drilling for water with a mud puncher, which had gone down about 40 metres, when he felt a soft sponginess and the drill rods dropped quickly. The drills ground through the earth's rock and when he pulled the rods to the surface they brought flesh and blood to the surface with them.

Norm, who had lived in the bush most of his life, said, 'I pulled up several kilograms of what appeared to be hide and flesh. It was definitely some sort of animal that had died a long time ago. There was a lot of animal flesh and beautiful brown hair, like fur. I went to Mum Hawke's place at Top Springs [the closest roadhouse to Killarney] and sent a wire to Darwin. A policeman came out and took a couple of tobacco tins of samples off me and sent them to Darwin.'

The material was sent to Adelaide for testing but a report from the Institute of Medical and Veterinary Science – reported in the *Sunday Territorian* – failed to shed any light on the mystery. It said that no recent human material was contained in the sample and no recognisable animal tissue was present. An examination of the hair-like material was also inconclusive but the report commented that 'the material resembled jute fibres'.

Norm decided to close the bore hole with a metal cap and moved 100 metres away to drill another bore, which yielded a good water flow. The new location was appropriately named Monster Bore. Norm always believed that he had found a prehistoric animal that had been preserved during the Ice Age. Because of this no one liked to camp at Monster Bore when mustering in the area – everyone was superstitious about the place!

Unlike the famous Lasseter's lost gold reef in Central Australia – which two of my uncles set out on an expedition to find in the early 1970s – the mysterious Ice Age animal of Monster Bore at Killarney Station has not attracted further attention from monster hunters, so we will never know what creature the fur and flesh belonged to.

•

A lot of the stories I heard when I was young were from the stockmen who would mostly talk about their droving trips – 'when I was a kid we drove 1000 kilometres with 1000 head of cattle' – and tales about their fights in a pub, their drinking feats or how their best horse had died. Storytelling was integral to our social gatherings. There was much that the Aboriginal people couldn't talk about, especially in mixed company, but they told stories about tracking lost people or tracking horses or finding a waterhole. These stories fascinated me, and I learnt a lot about bush life.

One of the stockmen was Freddy Holtze, a brother-in-law to Nancy Holtze, who came to Killarney as a housekeeper. Freddy was a happy, guitar-playing member of the Stolen Generation. Freddy changed his name to his stage name, 'Brasso Jackson'. He loved to play country songs by Freddy Fender and Charley Pride, and said he was going to save his money and go to Nashville, Tennessee in the United States of America. He instilled in me a love of country music and taught me how to play the guitar and sing Tammy Wynette, Skeeter Davis, Patsy Cline and Dolly Parton songs.

Australian country and western legends Slim Dusty and Joy McKean were our idols and we knew every song word for word. We travelled to the Top Springs Road House one year to see Slim Dusty perform live. For us this was like seeing The Beatles, who had taken the world by storm around the same time. I first heard of The Beatles when my cousin Robyn came down from Darwin for the school holidays with a record. I fell instantly in love with Paul McCartney, as did millions of other girls across the world.

My grandmother Lillian Tindill, who owned the frock shop in Katherine, sent Robyn and me a pair of white underpants with a black and white photo of The Beatles across the back for a Christmas present. I loved those knickers so much. How I wish I still had them!

•

Mum's brother Boko (real name Francis) had started working for Bill Tapp just before Bill Tapp met my mother, and he continued to live and work at Killarney after Mum moved there. He was a lovable larrikin who sang and laughed a lot. On one occasion after a drinking session at the nearby road house at Top Springs – an outback service station, pub and store – Boko returned very happily drunk and jumped on Bill Tapp's horse, which was saddled and waiting under a shady tree. He pulled the Luger rifle out of the saddle holster and fired a few shots into the air, just as if he was in a John Wayne movie, setting 500 head of cattle into a panic as they scattered and galloped through our camp.

The cattle trampled over swags and through the camp fires, knocking over buckets of precious water, billycans and tables of food. Mum, Daisy and Dora were running, screaming, and dragging all the kids behind trees, while the stockmen were galloping up and down the creek trying to get the cattle under control. When the stampede was over, the camp looked like a cyclone had gone through it and everyone was fuming.

Bill Tapp dragged Boko off the horse by the scruff of the neck and gave him a good dressing down, saying how people could have been trampled to death, not to mention they now had to muster half the mob of cattle still galloping in terror across the plains.

Boko was a little sedate for a few days but it was not long before his mischievous personality returned and he continued to be the life of the camp.

•

The terrain at Killarney is very flat and we could see the red dust trails or the headlights of vehicle hours before they got to the station. The lights, however, were not always as they seemed.

A Min Min light is a glowing disc of light that hovers just metres above the ground. It follows you, never gaining or losing the distance between you and it. I was alerted to this phenomenon by the stockmen who said they had seen Min Min lights when droving in Queensland or across the Barkly Tableland in the Northern Territory.

These stories were not told with a fear factor but as a statement of fact. I didn't question them as I gained much traditional wisdom through living so closely and in tune with the land and its people. I am not sure what the explanation for them is, but on a couple of occasions we saw Min Min lights while travelling to or from the station on very clear, brisk nights. The light would stop when you stopped to open a gate and then maintain the same distance as the car moved along the road. Spooky but not scary!

16 Killarney's Cattle

Very little had been written down about the country and cattle in the Victoria River district when Bill Tapp bought Killarney in 1960, so no one was sure how many cattle were on the station. The previous owners had estimated that there were approximately 5000 to 7000 head of wild cattle spread across the property.

Bill Tapp's first small muster yielded almost 1400 head of cattle and three-quarters of them were clean-skins, which was the name used for cattle who were unbranded and, therefore, unclaimed. All the clean-skin cattle automatically belonged to Killarney once they'd been mustered and this proved to be our good fortune – it was most likely there were a lot more than the estimated 5000 head of unclaimed cattle. As the country had never been fully mustered, the estimates were made on general stocking numbers across properties in the region.

The cattle were feral, and the markets were a long way from Killarney. Branding was carried out on a bronco panel, made from thick curved tree branches, hand-cut into wooden posts and placed deep in the ground. This provided a frame to pull the beast up against, which was then flipped over on its side for branding.

Bill Tapp would rope the clean-skins around the head from the back of his horse and drag them to the panel. The rope was secured to the saddle. The Aboriginal stockmen worked the leg ropes, catching a front and back leg to pull the beast off balance and onto its side.

As soon as the beast hit the ground, another man would pounce onto the horns to hold the head down. The Killarney ITH brand – from the names of Killarney's former owners, Eric Izod and Ivor Townshend Hall – was burnt onto every clean hide that came through the cattle yards and each beast was earmarked with the numeral 7. Each cattle station had a different shape of earmark so that cattle could be easily identified from a distance. Branded cattle from neighbouring properties were returned to their owners. Most of the bulls were scrawny, tough and wild, so were castrated to grow into bullocks for the markets, and the branded cows were sent back out to the paddocks to breed with breeding bulls selected by Bill Tapp.

Wild horses were rounded up and broken in for riding. Each person in the stock camp would be allocated four to six horses so they could be rotated each work day and if any were lame or hurt they could be left aside until they recovered. If you had fifteen stockmen this meant you had to have a camp of at least ninety horses as well as the pack mules. As the old horses were retired, new ones had to be broken.

There were no horse yards and very few fences, so the horses were cared for by the horse tailor, who knew every horse intimately. He fed them and hobbled them out at night with a small chain attached to two leather straps buckled around the horse's front legs to slow it down and inhibit it from wandering too far from the camp. At night, bells were placed around the horses' necks. The bells helped the horse tailor find the horses in the early morning for mustering. Mules were broken in and trained to carry pack saddles filled with food, water, swags, cooking gear and tools.

Everyone rose before sunrise while the cook stoked the fire up. The stockmen rolled out of their swags and prepared for another long, hot day in the saddle, after packing up the mules to carry water and food. The battle for survival for the cattle was as hard as it was for the people who lived out in the middle of nowhere trying to tame and bring the herd under control. During the dry season, cattle grew weak and got bogged, perishing on the edge of dried-up waterholes, their eyes picked out by crows. The cattle were infested with ticks that sucked their blood and energy, and bush flies scavenged around their eyes.

There were generally about six big musters and six small musters a year, covering an area of the station where the cattle gathered around waterholes. The stock camp workers would ride out to camp at one of the bores or waterholes and work the cattle back into a purpose-built paddock over a period of two or three days. They would then walk the mob 20 or 30 kilometres back to the main cattle yards at the station to be sorted and branded. These musters could yield up to 1000 head of cattle at a time.

With each round of mustering and branding, the herd that Killarney owned increased and some were sent off to the meatworks in Katherine.

Very early on Bill Tapp was clear about having to breed horses to suit the climate and the harsh conditions of the Territory. He bought a thoroughbred stallion called Basalt. Basalt was sired by a stallion called Star Kingdom and a dam (mother) called Boxilla. Basalt's blood lines came from superior imported breeds in Ireland and he was a great grandson of Hyperion, who ran in the 1935 Melbourne Cup.

Bill Tapp bought the stallion in 1962 to add height and longer legs and bring finer bone and finesse to the breeding stock of thick-set stock horses in the Territory. He raced the stallion once in Katherine, where he won his race, and on return to Killarney put him with a select group of mares. Basalt's time at Killarney was short: he came to a tragic end when he was bitten by a king brown snake and died. He had sired a few foals and Bill Tapp kept the females for the foundation of his breeding stock until he bought another stallion.

Following the death of Basalt, Bill Tapp continued to research the breeds and blood lines that he thought would best suit the Territory. Eventually, in 1969, he settled on the Quarter Horse, an imported American horse that was bred for its intelligence around cows, quiet personality and strong constitution in harsh conditions.

Elders GM, an agribusiness company that loaned money to farmers and cattle station owners, opened its first office in the Northern Territory in Katherine in 1968 because of the amount of work created by Bill Tapp on Killarney Station. They saw the opportunities to do business with the booming cattle industry and financed a wide range of spending sprees for new buildings, bores and fencing, vehicles, stud cattle and horses, trucks and helicopters, as well as providing the supplies at the station store with food, tobacco and alcohol.

In 1969, Bill Tapp flew south to the King Ranch bull sale in Bowral New South Wales, to purchase new blood lines for the cattle herd. He paid the Australian record price of $20 000 for an 18-month-old Santa Gertrudis bull: King Ranch Oregon, who became the foundation of a herd of over 30 000 head of cattle.

At the same sale, he paid an Australian record price of $12 000 for a Quarter Horse stallion, Quarter Commando. Bill Tapp believed that a Quarter Horse was more suitable to the harsh Territory conditions than the predominantly thoroughbred blood lines. Quarter Commando was the foundation sire for the station horses and Killarney Station was to become the biggest privately owned Quarter Horse stud in the world at the time.

The arrival of King Ranch Oregon and Quarter Commando brought out the whole station to watch them being unloaded from the truck. Bill Tapp led the gleaming chestnut stallion around, pointing out his regal head with its white blaze down the centre, and his thick, muscular body made for the harsh Territory conditions.

King Ranch Oregon was just a baby at eighteen months of age, but was soon put to work in a paddock full of specially selected cows. Oregon died after a good twenty years of service and was buried in a big hole near the bough shed where he spent his last days, close to the water and where Bill Tapp could see him outside the kitchen window every day.

17 The Cattle Yards and Our Head Stockman

The cattle yards were central to our existence on the station. They were our school and our playground, where we learnt not only about cattle and horses but also about people, respect and hard work.

I loved the smell of the yards, the thick, soupy dust and fresh, warm cow dung. I loved the smell of the burning hair that filled our nostrils when the branding iron singed its symbols into the cowhides. I loved the sounds of the cattle shuffling and snuffling at night, the cows calling in low voices for their babies.

The cattle yard was where we were given our first horse to ride, where our saddles were neatly lined up on a long wooden rail, bridle and saddlecloth thrown over them to keep the sun off. It was where the saddler worked, threading long curved needles with waxed string, cutting strips of leather into hobble straps, stitching bridles, making new stirrup leathers with carefully measured holes for the buckles.

The horse tailor brought the horses to the cattle yard every day and tended to their care, painting their sore backs with purple iodine and smearing their eyes with black tar to keep the swarming flies away. The horses would stand patiently, waiting for their iron shoes to be heated on the red-hot coals and shaped on the anvil and then nailed on to their hooves to protect them from cutting their feet on the sharp rocks.

The cattle yard was also where the horse-breaker broke in the new colts every wet season. Each horse hurled himself against the rails in confusion, eyes wild as the breaker threw the rope around his neck, talking, soothing and patting him to quieten him down.

The stockmen would buck out the newly broken colt as the onlookers yelled and cooeed, the rider hanging on for dear life to avoid being speared into the thick bull dust.

The cattle yard was where you had to wear the right uniform: blue jeans, R.M. Williams boots, a leather belt carved with your name and fastened by a shiny horseshoe buckle, long-sleeved blue shirt and an akubra hat. None of that fancy American stuff like in the movies!

The cattle yard was no place for tears or tantrums. It was where you were teased mercilessly for opening the gate too soon or too late; where you were labelled a sook if you cried for being slammed into the gate; where everyone howled with laughter if you were trampled into the dirt by a crazy cow.

In the yard, the young bulls were run into the long wooden crush, castrated and earmarked, then had their horns blunted with a saw. The stockmen rode the bulls out of the crush to practise their rodeo skills, the bulls jumping and twisting, horns swinging wildly, snot and blood flying as one of the other stockmen tormented them to make the bullock buck harder.

The stockmen liked to sit on the top rail for a smoko break, concentrating deeply as they slowly rolled the tobacco through their hands, cigarette paper hanging out of the corner of the mouth, eyes squinting through the dust. They bragged about throwing bulls, riding a buck jumper or the last drinking spree in town. They talked about their dreams, buying a new car, saving enough money to go south to see their mother, of getting a head stockman's job or buying their own cattle station.

The government-employed stock inspectors were an extended part of the camp and spent days at a time on the station testing for diseases, and applying bush vet surgery to help deliver calves, give injections and provide ointments and bandages for cuts and fly-bitten eyes. They tested for botulism and brucellosis and dipped the cattle for ticks.

The person who taught me so much about cattle and country was our head stockman, Sandy Shaw, who came to work for us in the 1960s. He was a part-Aboriginal man whose white father had been a saddler travelling through the region repairing saddles on the stations in the 1930s. Sandy had a younger brother, Ringer Shaw, and they were both born at the neighbouring Victoria River Downs Station to their Aboriginal mother, Lily Anzac. Sandy was the eldest of the children and his mother went on to have many more children to her traditional husband.

Sandy existed across two worlds: he lived with his Aboriginal family when he was a little boy, then, following his initiation and rites of passage according to tribal law at about the age of thirteen, he was sent to work in the stock camp. He was taught basic reading and writing while cattle droving with the white drovers who travelled the region delivering cattle to the meatworks and sale yards.

Sandy was blind in one eye, which he said was caused by a gun backfiring and exploding near his face when he was a young man. He also had a large, unfinished tribal scar that reached halfway across his upper chest, unlike the ones of the other men such as Georgie and Banjo, who had two or three lines that reached right across their chests. The scar looked as if it had been brought to an abrupt end; however, I never asked Sandy how or why this had happened. It was common for most of the men to have at least two or three tribal scars across their chests and along their upper arms. It was men's business and never discussed.

Sandy walked tall and proud, and was a softly spoken, gentle man. He never married or had children and he treated Billy and me like his own. He showed us how to ride properly and take care of our horses and saddles, how to plait a belt and make green hide ropes. When we were allowed to go out to the stock camp at night, we slept in our swags beside him, away from the rest of the stockmen.

He loved country music and had a little transistor radio with a long wire aerial that he threw up into a tree to listen to the country and western radio show from Mt Isa, Queensland. People from stations and road camps across the Top End wrote in requesting that their favourite song be played, and sent messages to family and friends. This was one of the highlights of our lives, as we learnt new songs, heard old songs and, on a very rare occasion, heard a message for someone at Killarney.

Sandy happily passed on his bush skills to the many young stockmen who came and went. He knew how to break in a wild horse, castrate a bull, make saddles and bridles and plait beautiful belts and whips. He knew how to mend a fence and fix a bore, how to change a tyre and drive a truck. He had a deep understanding of the land, and compassion and respect for the people around him.

When we went mustering, Sandy would show us what tracks belonged to which animal and how to tell if the tracks were old or new. He would kneel in the dirt and trace the track gently with a finger.

'See the sharp edges of this goanna track, that means they are new tracks, maybe about two or three hours old, and he is going for a drink at the creek. See these horse tracks, the edges are smoothed by the wind and they are underneath the goanna track so they are older, maybe the horses went for a drink early in the morning, before the goanna woke up.'

As we walked along behind the cattle, Sandy would tell us stories of when he was a little boy and how he had learnt to ride, track and mend saddles. He would talk about droving and the people he had met along the way. He had a wicked sense of humour and told fascinating stories of mad cooks, drovers and wild horses.

What seemed to me to be very cruel – stories of fighting with sticks and boomerangs and the payback system of spearing people for their misdemeanours – also gave me an awareness and understanding at a young age of the complexities and rituals of another culture. I feel blessed and privileged that I had the opportunity to be included in a way most Australians are not. This was also due to my mother liking and enjoying the company of the Aboriginal people who lived with us on the station. We were not segregated, as per the social expectations of those times. We had sleepovers at the camp and the Aboriginal kids had sleepovers at our house.

Generally, though, Sandy spoke little about his traditional life, nor did he mix with the full-blood Aboriginal people on the station. He loved to read paperback Western novels featuring 'Larry and Stretch' and listen to Slim Dusty and Charley Pride country songs on a tape recorder. I don't recall him leaving the station much to visit his family. Like so many people who came to work there, Killarney was his home.

18 Communicating with the Outside World

We kids learnt about the cycles of life on Killarney. Cattle were killed for us to eat, and they died for other reasons too. They perished in dams, and died while giving birth, from heat exhaustion, from tuberculosis or tick fever, or from being mauled by dingoes. Life and death were raw and exposed. This random aspect of life was brought more starkly to reality with human tragedy, when Mum's brother Boko drowned in the Katherine River during the wet season of March 1963, when he was seventeen years old. He had gone to town to see Nana at a time when the Katherine River was in flood. He and a group of friends were swimming in the swirling brown waters near the Low Level bridge when his girlfriend became caught in an undertow. Boko jumped into the flooding river to save her, but he hit his head on the weir and disappeared out of sight. The whole town searched for him all night, but it wasn't until the following morning that he was found a few hundred metres downriver by his brother Jim.

The message of Boko's death was delivered to my mother by the Salvation Army minister, Captain Victor Pedersen, who flew his little Tiger Moth plane out to Killarney for the purpose. It was too wet to land, so he flew low over the house a couple of times, waving a white rag to alert us that he had a message. He then dropped a note wrapped around a rock the size of a cricket ball.

Bill Tapp had left on horseback with some of the Aboriginal men that morning, taking a pack mule and swags to mend broken fences and muster some cattle on the way home, so Mum sent our mechanic to deliver the news to him. The message Mum's brother had died was also delivered over Radio VJY, so everyone in the district was aware of the tragic accident.

With the wet season well and truly set in, the road was too wet and boggy for Mum to get to town. She wasn't able to attend her youngest brother's funeral or be there to comfort her mother. It was another lesson for me in how much the seasons of the Territory affected our lives, for bad as well as good. The wet season could be as dangerous as the dry season, in very different ways. It wasn't the first time that the Wet had claimed a victim, or kept someone from attending something important. It wouldn't be the last, either. I would keep finding that out, year after year, on Killarney.

There were no transport or freight services to Killarney so food, medical essentials and mail were picked up when a truck was sent to town. Shopping trips were always put off until the last moment, such as when food supplies were getting dangerously low or vital parts were needed for bores and vehicles.

One mid-1960s wet season we were going on a rare trip to Katherine for some Christmas shopping, only to get caught on Battle Creek, a notorious creek crossing on Killarney about 30 kilometres from the homestead. The truck lost traction going up a steep riverbank and kept slipping back into the river, which was running about halfway up the tyres. Mum, who was pregnant again and could not swim, was pulling us off the back of the truck onto the bank as the truck slipped further towards the river before gently settling in the water.

As the sun was setting, it was clear we weren't going anywhere that day. Bill Tapp set up a tarpaulin strung off a tree on the side of the road and Mum settled for the evening with a couple of pillows and a blanket with her gaggle of tired, sunburnt and hungry kids crawling all over her. As the dank, dark wet-season night settled in, we tried to sleep under the little tarp in the pouring rain while being bombarded by mosquitoes as big as birds. It was a long, restless night of babies crying and trying to get comfortable on the hard ground.

The truck was finally leveraged out of the river in the clear light of day and we headed off to town. But just a kilometre or so short of the main road, we not only got bogged again but the battery on the truck died. No amount of digging or cranking the engine was going to help this situation.

Bill Tapp sent a very faint message through Radio VJY to ask them to contact Killarney and tell someone to bring a tractor, battery and jumper leads out to us. After he sent the message he started to walk back home because the radio reception was so bad he wasn't sure that the message had got through. He had walked about 15 kilometres when he was finally met by a couple of the men on the tractor.

Mum waited patiently, covered in the usual haze of black flies, under a little tree while we played cowboys and Indians with stick guns around anthills. The survival kit Mum always carried was our lifeline: we subsisted on black tea and a tin of Sunshine Milk to mix with the dirty red-brown water from the creek, a few tins of spaghetti and baked beans, and a packet of Sao biscuits. She hadn't anticipated that what would normally be about a six-hour drive was going to take over two days and nights to complete.

Once we finally arrived, my nana's house – with its warm showers, clean beds and food – was, by far, better than any Christmas present.

The radio telephone service replaced the two-way radio as the main source of communication in the early 1970s. One could only use the radio telephone for a maximum of twelve minutes and this conversation was interrupted every three minutes with a voice out of the ether: 'Three minutes, sir, are you extending?' the voice would say.

'Y-y-yyesss p-p-p-please,' Bill Tapp would reply.

He always went over the twelve minutes and drove the telephonists mad as he asked for further extensions. He told the women at the radio telephone exchange that he should have extra time because he stuttered.

19 Raining Fish and Life in the Wet

Banjo was a 'rain man' and he carried small pieces of sparkling quartz rock tied up in a red-spotted bandana and used these to sing the rain; we also placed large pieces of quartz under dripping pipes and taps to encourage the rain. To 'sing something into existence' is a common Aboriginal concept passed down over generations. The song is often in the form of a chant and is associated with a material object such as a quartz stone, a bone, or strands of hair.

I'm sure Banjo's innate knowledge of the country and seasons contributed to his success rate of 'singing the rain' when the big storms came rolling in. I didn't question his ability to do this. There are things, phenomena, that just are.

The build-up was also when the mango trees bore their fruit. My nana would send us mangoes from Katherine, where the trees were plentiful and the fruit would rot on the ground if it wasn't eaten or sent to hungry mouths like ours. We feasted on so many mangoes that we always got mango sores, a burn around the mouth from the high, acidic, vitamin C content.

During the build-up, the ants scurried to build their red hills and the kangaroos waited on black soil plains, looking towards the sky. The cattle stayed close to the bores and drying dams, and the stockmen burnt little piles of dry manure in the cattle yards to create a thick smoke to keep the flies away from the horses' eyes.

Little orange-striped hornets hung over the puddles, gathering mud to build their nests under eaves, tables and chairs at the homestead. Green frogs would come out of nowhere, millions of them, singing loudly in the down pipes.

When the clouds finally burst, we would run out into the rain in our underpants, screaming with joy while throwing the red mud at each other, smearing it all over our bodies and in our hair and dancing like the Indians we saw in Hollywood movies. The stockmen would throw their hats in the air and the old Aboriginal women would stand out in the rain, smiling and swaying.

Bill Tapp would stand on the verandah, dark clouds almost visibly lifting from his shoulders because he did not have to worry about the cattle dying around the rapidly drying waterholes, or bore pumps breaking down.

One wet season we headed out for a rain dance. We jumped, squealed and slid in the mud, throwing mud balls at each other. There were thousands of little silver fish, no more than an inch long, flapping all over the ground and we ran around picking them up by the handful. We raced home, fists and knickers full of fish.

'Muuuuum, it's raining fish, it's raining fish!'

'Stay outside, you kids,' she admonished us. 'Don't come in here covered in all that mud.'

Bill Tapp came to check out the commotion and found a mob of kids all lining up with hands full of fish. Before we knew it, everyone was out, looking at thousands of little silver fish flapping on the red ground and in mud puddles. In true Bill Tapp fashion, he wanted to save as many as possible – hating to see any animal harmed – and we had to pick up as many as we could and put them in the water tanks and the troughs.

The raining fish phenomenon occurred a number of times – to this day it is not an unusual occurrence in the Victoria River region. It seems that, through a quirk of nature, the fish hatchlings can be swept up in a wind squall over a river and dumped hundreds of kilometres away by the rain.

●

Every year, after the first rains, Bill Tapp loaded all the Aboriginal residents onto the back of the truck to take them back to Wave Hill Station for their initiation ceremonies and to deliver young wives to their promised husbands. Billy and I loved to go on these trips. Daisy, Dora, Banjo and Georgie sat on swags in the back of the truck, all their worldly goods wrapped in old dresses piled up high along with the newly made nulla nullas, boomerangs and spears for ceremonies and trading, and to be given as presents to family.

Billy and I preferred to be in the back, with the wind blowing through our hair as Daisy and Dora chattered excitedly in language about going back to the country to see their families. It must have been thrilling for the old ladies, who only saw their extended families during the wet season gatherings. It was a time for them to talk to their daughters and meet their new grandchildren, nieces and nephews; a time to share stories and sort out family problems.

The road to Wave Hill was a precarious trip of over 250 kilometres of rocky ridges and steep creek beds. The truck was old and rattly, and if we weren't bogged in mud we were bogged in bull dust, or broken down with a leaky radiator or flat tyre. We would wait on the side of the road until someone came by to help or until the bush mechanics fixed the problem. I was good at carrying rocks and logs to stack under the tyres to help provide grip in the mud or dust. The old ladies would look for bush bananas, berries and wild honey.

On one of the wet season treks returning from Wave Hill in an empty truck, we got bogged to the axles and couldn't move. My cousin Robyn and I were about ten years old at that time and Billy was eight. After hours of trying to chock the truck up with logs and anthills, it sank deeper into the soft earth. There was only Bill Tapp with us three little kids, and we could not provide the muscle power needed to push the truck out.

It was unlikely that someone would come driving by anytime soon, so Bill Tapp decided we should walk back to a construction camp near the road house at Top Springs to get help. Bare-footed and wearing only shorts, we walked all afternoon, stopping at creeks to cool off and picking wild berries and sour paddymelons along the way.

We finally arrived at the construction camp at sundown, starving and badly sunburnt. The camp was empty. We had walked through 20 kilometres of mud in the heat of the day and our feet were raw.

Robyn was suffering from severe heat stroke and was running a temperature. Billy had large watery blisters all over his nose and shoulders. We made ourselves at home in an old silver caravan set up as a kitchen and ate tins of bully beef and baked beans before falling asleep in another caravan set up with beds.

We spent the night in the camp and the following morning walked another five kilometres into Top Springs to send a radio message home for someone to come and pick us up. The construction workers from the camp were sympathetic and bought us cold drinks and lollies.

The Wet often had an impact on how we would spend our Christmas and we had to do a big store order for goods that would last at least three months because once the rains set in we couldn't leave the station. One year, a truck loaded with thousands of dollars' worth of these food stores and Christmas presents was swept off a bridge into a raging river a week before Christmas. On the way home from Katherine, the driver, Ivan Woods, became impatient waiting for the rushing water to drop low enough to drive across. Ivan and his mate, deaf Kenny Wesley, waited, despondent and embarrassed, on the side of the road for hours, watching the swollen river gush over the top of the truck, until they were picked up by another traveller. The neighbours finally came and winched the vehicle out of the river.

The groceries, tobacco, matches, Christmas cakes, fresh fruit and hams, Santa stockings and gifts, along with bags of sugar and flour, were all fish food at the bottom of the river. Anything that was retrievable, such as tinned food, was saved. More Christmas presents and perishables were ordered over the two-way radio and another vehicle went to town to pick them up. Somehow Santa managed to find his way along the boggy roads and arrive in the early hours of Christmas morning.

Ivan and Kenny were not the most popular people on the station that Christmas, but at least the tinned food, beer and rum were saved. We laughed for years afterwards when Ivan told the story of how he and Kenny surfaced after crawling out of the sinking truck's windows, only for Kenny to immediately jump straight back into the raging river. When he didn't come up, Ivan went after him and hauled him out of the water. Kenny fought against him, yelling, 'I've got to get my rum, my rum, MY RUM!' He dived back into the river and managed to salvage the bottle of rum that was hidden behind the car seat.

Despite the hard times, the wet season signalled a time of festivities and fun. No matter how wet it got or how many vehicles were broken down and how many roads we had to walk, Santa always made it to Killarney. The Santa sack got bigger and heavier with each passing year as our family continued to grow. Santa always managed to leave at least one brightly wrapped present under the scrawny tree branch propped in a flour drum wrapped in faded Christmas paper, with a dusty, broken-winged angel on the top. No matter how low the food stores got, Mum always came up with a rich Christmas cake with white icing and plastic holly on top, a big hot roast dinner, and pudding that concealed silver threepenny and sixpenny coins and was covered with creamy yellow custard.

Christmases were always shared with those who had nowhere to go over the wet season. The Aboriginal families joined in and my mother made sure that there were presents for everyone. The men got bottles of aftershave lotion and a packet of cigarettes. The women received perfumes and pretty costume jewellery. Old Micko the cook would recite 'My Brother Ben and I', perched up on a flour drum with his little pink towelling hat, white singlet, shorts and odd-coloured thongs. The table was piled high with delicious food, pannikins of rum and homemade cordial. Sitting on chairs made from tree stumps and empty upturned flour drums in the heat and rain, we sang Christmas carols and shared homemade presents.

It was the tradition on Boxing Day for all the women and kids to go swimming down the creek. And then, with the festivities over, it was back to work for everyone.

20 Camping

The whole 2819 square kilometres of Killarney was our home. Even though we had the homestead, we regularly camped in different locations, near waterholes or bores, to trap, muster and brand the wild cattle. One of our favourite spots to camp was at Companion Springs.

Companion Springs was on the far western boundary, close to the Top Springs Road House, where we were able to buy lollies and cold drinks when driving past. Companion was a picturesque area with a series of cool waterholes along the creek sheltered by large paperbark trees. We camped on the banks with a large tarpaulin strung between some large trees to serve as the kitchen and main living area. There was an open fireplace with a corrugated-iron fire break on the side of the prevailing winds. The fireplace had the billycans of tea, large tubs of corned beef and a hole for an in-ground oven, filled with hot rocks and coals.

We made Companion Springs our last muster for the year, as it was the last of the creeks that had water while we waited for the first rains. It was easy to trap cattle and horses at that time of year as they had to come in to water every day. There was a 'trap paddock', a fenced area around the waterhole with a 'spear gate', made of wooden rails that were built in a V shape that allowed the cattle to squeeze through to enter the water hole, but they could not get out as the spear-headed end was narrow and had sharp ends preventing them from leaving.

Our camp was located just a kilometre off the Buchanan Highway, the road that joined the Victoria Highway and travelled through Victoria River Downs and on to Timber Creek. The word 'highway' is a bit grand for what it was in those days – a corrugated graded single-lane dirt road maintained by the NT Department of Transport. However, this location also meant that we had more regular visitors than we would get at the end of the 42-kilometre road into Killarney. Due to the massive area of the Victoria River Downs Station, there was an outstation called Moolooloo about 15 kilometres away from our camp, so we would get visits from the manager and stockmen.

On one occasion while camped at Companion Springs, Mum and Bill Tapp had gone for a drive to check the trap paddocks about 30 kilometres away and left us with Old Dora and Daisy. They had taken my baby brother Sam with them and left Billy and my three-year-old sister, Shing, who was regularly contained in a large meat-safe cot to save her from walking to the creek or into the fire.

Billy, Nita and I were playing around the fire making johnnycakes. Shing, who was skinny with a tangle of wind-blown, knotted blonde hair, was crying in the cot to get out. I lifted her out to keep her quiet and we continued to make our little johnnycakes, covering them in sticky golden syrup and eating them.

All of a sudden I heard a wrenching scream – Shing had stepped into the fire! I pulled her out, threw her on my hip and started running towards Daisy and Dora at the creek. Within minutes Shing's foot was covered in huge, ballooning blisters filled with fluid. She was screaming and I was terrified. Daisy took her and immediately started rubbing fat into the burn, which was the remedy used at the time.

Shing cried for hours and there was nothing we could do but wait for Mum and Bill Tapp to return. When they finally came back to the camp they took Shing to the Top Springs Road House to get treatment for the burns. Though my parents didn't blame me, I felt terribly guilty for many years, because I was the one who took her out of the cot. The burns were quite severe and she had to be taken into Katherine Hospital, but Shing soon recovered, and while she only vaguely remembers the incident, she still has the scars on her foot.

The old Aboriginal ladies always came with us and set up camp under trees not far from where our family camped when mustering. Mum allowed me to go to the camp at night and I loved the smell of the fire and the bits of meat sizzling on the coals and the black tea. The women spent the days washing clothes in the creeks and looking after the kids. Long into the night they would sit on their swags, talking and laughing and singing. Dora, in her strong voice, and Daisy, in her high, sweet voice, would sing together for hours on end. These festive occasions tended to occur when we killed a cow for the weekly supply of beef, or when one of the boys had brought back a big bush turkey or goanna and there was plenty of meat to feast on.

Big logs would be thrown on the fire so that the flames were leaping into the night and the goanna – skin, guts and all – was tossed onto the bonfire. The skin sizzled, crackled and curled, and the women licked their lips in delight as they turned the big lizard backwards and forwards over the flames. When he was cooked, Mr Goanna was laid on some fresh leaves to cool before Daisy would pull out a huge butcher knife and slit the reptile open, the cooked entrails spilling as she scooped out the kidneys and liver to be eaten. She hacked off the tail and pulled the skin back, revealing the white meat. She would then tear off big chunks for us to share.

After the meal was eaten, it was time for other things, such as teaching Nita and me the women's dances. 'Come, you young ones, you gotta dance now,' Dora would say. 'You got to learn to dance proper way.'

She would do a demo for us, with her bag foot shuffling in the dust, arms swinging in rhythm from side to side.

We would giggle and say, 'Noooo, we shame for doing that dance.'

Dora would continue to sing and sternly insist, 'No, you young girl, you come here, you got to learn to dance proper way.'

Dora prepared Nita to go to her promised husband at Montejinni Station by teaching her the dances and stories and the family spiritual songs to support her when she left. I didn't understand then that there was a clear time when Nita would go away, but one wet season she went on the ceremonial holidays and never returned. She took up her position as the third wife to Bill King Langandi at Montejinni Station. Her older sisters Mabel and Eileen were his first and second wives. I had lost my best friend and that was that – there was absolutely nothing anyone could do about it. Nita's fate had been set by ancient traditions before she was even born.

One of our favourite places to visit on Killarney was Gallery Hill, so named because of the Aboriginal paintings in the rock overhang. We often took visiting family, friends and dignitaries to have a look at the paintings, which had probably been made during the wet season, because the good supply of bush tucker when the rains came would have allowed families to live there for a while.

The rock paintings depict two magnificent Lightning Brothers, each about two metres tall, surrounded by drawings of kangaroos and goannas. The Lightning Brothers, spirits of the Wardaman people, are depicted in their full ceremonial headdresses, painted in red and white striped ochre. In the cave, on a ledge just above head height near the paintings, there were also the bones of a small child lying on pieces of paperbark.

We never touched the paintings or the bones and I hope that they remain as pristine as they were when I was a little girl standing in that big red rock cave, in awe of the people who travelled the vast dry lands, leaving behind their stories as large works of art.

21 Accidents Happen

While we ran wild and were adept at surviving in the harshest of conditions, it could be a dangerous life for all who lived there. My little brother Joe, aged about ten at the time, ended up in hospital after going for a drive in the back tray of the ute to check fences in the wet season. The kids loved going for a drive at any time for any reason, and it was fun in the wet season when you hit bog holes and the red mud flew over the roof and splattered in your face, or the car skidded back and forth on the road.

On this occasion there were about six little kids sitting on the back of the ute, laughing and skylarking, when the car slid into the wire fence, catching Joe's arm that was hanging over the edge. He screamed as the steel fence picket gouged out a large piece of flesh at the elbow and severed the artery in his left arm. The car came to a screeching halt and they wrapped the wound tightly in a sweat-covered shirt and sped back to the station.

The doctor was called on the radio telephone and Joe was given a large pannikin of rum to dull the pain while Mum awaited the arrival of the Flying Doctor an hour or so later.

On arrival in Katherine (after vomiting up the rum on the plane), Joe had his wound stitched and a minor skin graft applied. A few days later when Joe's arm was put under a ray lamp to dry the infection, he suffered third-degree burns. This meant the wound had to first heal and then another skin graft had to be done with skin from the top of his thigh.

Poor Joe spent almost three months in hospital. Our Aunty Jan was a nursing sister at the hospital and looked after him. Joe says that he thinks everyone forgot he was there, as he never got a visit from our parents or any of the Killarney staff in that time. The nurses entertained him and he fattened up on the 'flash' food served by the hospital. Soups, chicken, fresh vegetables, ice cream, 'town bread' and butter replaced the diet of beef and vegetables three times a day, seven days a week. Eventually he was picked up by the truck driver and returned home to Killarney.

Life certainly could be precarious for the kids of Killarney. One school holiday Bill Tapp asked Billy to climb up the radio telephone tower and check if there were broken wires, as the phone wasn't working and the galahs had a tendency to get into the plastic-coated wires and chew at them. Billy was about fourteen years old at the time, nimble and a lightweight.

We were all standing under the thin tower swaying in the wind as Billy reached the top and let out a scream. He had grabbed hold of the powerline that had been stripped by the galahs.

Mum was yelling at Bill Tapp and I was watching in terror when, miraculously, Billy managed to pull himself free from the electrical current. My brother shakily descended to earth to reveal that the wire had seared a cut right to the bone of his finger. He didn't come off too much the worse for wear in the end, and though it could have had a tragic ending, he was happy to retell the story and show the evidence of the blackened skin seared on his forefinger.

We had to contend with wild bulls, floods and bushfires, not to mention the creepy-crawlies. One of the world's deadliest and most dangerous snakes, the king brown, scorpions and redback spiders also lurked around our home. We had many encounters with king browns getting into buildings, gardens, woodheaps, the chook house, under saddles and feed bags, and on one occasion slithering into the office under the feet of my mother and the cook. The cook and Mum flew up onto the chairs, screaming for someone to come and get the snake. The distress call was answered by Ivan Woods, the daredevil snake-catcher, who managed to hold the snake's head down with a long stick while grabbing it by the tail and yanking it out the door, swinging it around his head to slam it on the ground and kill it. The snake was so big and heavy he let it go in mid-air and it went flying, turning around and around for what seemed like forever. We all took off in every direction as it hurtled back to earth. The snake landed and was stunned long enough for Ivan to finish it off with a shovel. It was over three metres long.

Redback spiders, centipedes and scorpions could be found under beds, in boxes, under chairs and in the toilet. One New Year's Day we were all at the men's kitchen having lunch when my then three-year-old sister Caroline – born in 1968 – was bitten by a redback when she put her foot into an old boot. She was screaming in agony and I hurled her onto my hip and raced down to our house, about 500 metres through the mud. We called the doctor on the radio telephone but there was nothing else we could do as the roads to town were cut off. The doctor said the most important thing was to not let her fall asleep. We did not have any major painkillers suitable for a child in the medicine kit, so we just had to sit it out and hope she wouldn't die. The doctor called back every half an hour to get an update and to talk us through the incident. Caroline must have been a tough little thing because after hours of crying and a very swollen red knee where you could see the red line of the poisoned vein travelling up her little leg, the pain began to ease and we let her go to bed. She was very sick for a few days but made it through. It is awful to feel so helpless, to be unable to do anything to ease the pain, and it was very scary in those first few hours.

My mother was bitten by a scorpion on her foot, which swelled to twice its size. A scorpion bite is incredibly painful; the pain lasts for days, and can recur for months. The head stockman, Sandy Shaw, a big man, was also bitten by a redback when he put a shirt on and the spider was inside the shirt. It bit him on the chest and the bite left him prostrate in bed for about three days in a high fever, moaning and drifting in and out of sleep with the pain.

Along with these deadly creatures, there were plenty of mosquitoes, bees, hornets, cattle ticks, bull ants and other insects with painful stings that were part of our daily life.

The travelling outback nursing sisters also covered the region, carrying out preventative health services to support the doctor visits. The sisters were based at Wave Hill Station, 250 kilometres west of Killarney, and they travelled on bush tracks, changing tyres and digging themselves out of bogs.

They came through Killarney about six times a year and set up their clinic on the back verandah of our house. They followed up on immunisations, weighed babies, looked after cuts and broken bones, and provided much-needed female contact for many station women.

One of our favourites was Sister Eileen Jones, the leprosy sister, whose area covered the whole of the north end of the Northern Territory. Sister Eileen had a leg caliper – its necessity, I assume, caused by polio – and she was strong, bossy and resourceful. Sister Eileen travelled across the Top End treating people with the debilitating disease of leprosy that caused ulcers and sores that would not heal, documenting and recording the control of the disease and any new cases.

In addition, and more importantly for us kids, Sister Eileen always brought 'black cat' lollies and took lots of photos of us.

22 A Bush Education

My education was an erratic affair in the first few years, thanks to our numerous moves before setting up a permanent home. I learnt reading and writing from Mum as a day-to-day thing rather than from any formal lessons, until we were finally signed up to the South Australian Correspondence School when I was about seven or eight, and received structured sets of lessons that arrived in the mail every few months. At the time, the Northern Territory was governed by South Australia. We didn't have a regular mail service so relied on the Flying Doctor, travelling nurses and truck drivers to deliver the mail for us.

In our very first schoolroom we sat at a handmade table on empty upturned five-gallon kerosene tins. The school days were erratic as Mum had so much to do. I enjoyed the lessons from the Correspondence School, loved the simple drawings and lined pages, and took huge pride in the set exercises, adding up and taking away numbers in arithmetic, spelling words and writing their meaning beside them, and copying the cursive writing so they were an exact image of the ones on the sample page.

I also loved the compulsory readers; once I'd read them, they were sent off bearing my mother's signature to verify that I really had done the work. I always waited in great anticipation for the next lot. I consumed the stories featuring Dick, Dora, Nip and Fluff as fast as I could and before long was reading *Grimm's Fairy Tales*, Enid Blyton, *Black Beauty*, *Huckleberry Finn*, *The Arabian Nights* and *Sleeping Beauty* as well as the paperback cowboy and detective novellas that the stockmen read. My grandmother also helped by sending lots of children's books for us to read.

Mail day was one of the most exciting days on the station for me and I could not wait to get my schoolwork back. I loved to read the neatly written comments by the unknown teacher 3000 kilometres away in Adelaide. She would stamp pictures of koalas, echidnas, platypus and kangaroos and the words 'excellent' or 'well done' onto the completed work. She wrote encouraging sentences such as, 'This is a lovely story about the donkey eating all the bread. I look forward to hearing more.'

A regular contributor to our reading and writing material was the Salvation Army minister, Captain

Pedersen. When he flew his plane into Killarney, he'd always arrive with a supply of books and magazines for Mum, and colouring books with the stories from the Bible and pencils for us kids, along with a generous dose of the good Lord's word. We were given little cards of scriptures that we had to learn off by heart and recite to him on his next visit.

He only visited once or twice a year and though I kept the little cards, I'm not sure I ever remembered a single line. The captain was a kindly man who loved his work and who persevered with us, knowing that my mother was a proclaimed atheist and it was up to him to do everything he could to inject a little Christianity into our lives.

My parents must have decided that we needed more disciplined learning as Mum was so busy with station life, so they sent Billy and me to board with Uncle Rex and Aunty Pat in Darwin in 1964, when I was nine. They had two little boys, Alan and Colin.

Rex and Pat lived in a brick house in a seaside suburb and we attended Nightcliff Primary School. We were glad to still be with family, as there was that same sense of humour, that same sense of belonging, and that little safety net – although, looking back, I wonder why anyone would put their kids in a cattle truck and send them to Darwin for school!

I don't remember a great deal about that year in Darwin other than that we played a lot on the crushed-ant-bed tennis court in the backyard and rode bikes up and down the street, but I do remember that this was the time I learnt to love cheese and Vegemite sandwiches. I took to school with great enthusiasm and after a few weeks in Grade 1 to determine my level, I was placed in Grade 3.

Darwin was a sprawling tropical town with wide roads and houses built on stilts. One of the biggest community events at the time was the annual *NT News* Walkabout, which was a sixteen-mile-long walk that most of the Darwin population participated in. Leading up to the competition, Aunty Pat took us to the football oval every evening to walk around for at least an hour. On the day of the competition, we packed early to drive out of town to the starting line. I completed the full sixteen miles in bare feet, shedding my sandshoes very early in the race, and came first in my age group. I carried the little trophy I won everywhere.

Billy and I stayed the full year in Darwin but it may have been too stressful for my aunty, or maybe my parents weren't able to pay for us to continue to stay up there, so the following year we stayed at home the first half of the year, doing correspondence. But we were dropping behind, as Mum had so many children and too much to do on the station, so we were sent to Katherine to live with Mum's youngest sister, Sue, and her husband, Barry, to attend the Katherine Area School. I was moved straight into Grade 6, which caught me up with my age group. I loved the school and my classes. I kept my pencils sharp and wrote neat cursive words exactly within the lines, onto the crisp white pages of my schoolbooks. My love of school paid off and, at the end of the year, I was presented with a book as Dux of Grade 6. I still have that book, one of the few precious things I saved when our house was flooded in the Katherine Australia Day flood of 1998.

The time with Aunty Sue was great and we liked being in Katherine because we knew everyone and felt more at home; however, it was most likely a stressful time for her to have two wild bush kids in her house with a new husband and baby, so the following year we stayed on Killarney again. This suited Billy and me as we loved being home on the station.

During this time, Bill Tapp began to build a brick schoolhouse a few hundred metres away from our home. The schoolhouse had a small residence attached to it so my parents could employ a governess to cater for the growing student numbers being produced by my mother and the Aboriginal women.

Our ever-expanding family provided a sure line-up of new students for the schoolroom. My little sister Shing soon joined us. Shing perched on her kerosene drum on her first day of school, hair brushed and face clean to begin the first page of Set 1 for Grade 1. Mum read out all the instructions and explained what was to be done for the day. She told Shing to 'put a tick beside the right answer and a cross beside the wrong answer'.

Shing worked quietly and enthusiastically, as did Billy and me. Well, actually, I don't think Billy was ever enthusiastic and he only did the bare minimum so he could get out of the schoolroom as quickly as possible to go to the cattle yards.

Mum returned to check our work and asked Shing how she was coming along. Shing proudly displayed her beautifully completed page. Crosses were placed in all the appropriate boxes, and little round cattle ticks with eight legs and two eyes were neatly placed in all the remaining boxes. That was Shing's version of a tick and why would she think anything different? We laughed and laughed and retold the story many times. It is still one of our favourite family stories.

23 Our Own Governess

Our first governess, Beth Marsh, came to Killarney all the way from Brisbane. She was very strict and loved bush poetry. She also loved the bush life, so she settled well into the station. Billy and I would go riding with Beth, who was intent on teaching us to ride 'properly', meaning like city hack riders. We took no heed, of course, and continued to gallop around at full speed, legs and arms flailing. While she was instructing us about sitting up straight, keeping toes pointed to the front and the reins held just so, she would make us recite Banjo Paterson and Henry Lawson poems. Billy hated it and tried to avoid going riding with her whenever he could. I was not very keen either and while I tried my best to learn the poems, I also avoided riding with her as often as I could.

Beth lived in the new school complex, which, like our house, had dirt floors, no doors or windows, no electricity and no running water. She taught a class of about six children in the schoolroom, with its wooden bookcase, chest of drawers and blackboard on the wall. She was very strict, which didn't appeal to the boys at all. In fact, it meant the boys were always skipping school. They would go up to the yards at smoko time and not return.

Beth would complain to Bill Tapp and he would smile and give the kids a very lame lecture about the importance of school, but mostly he was to blame because he would give them some work while they were there and that provided an excuse not to return. A few hours at school in the morning were more than enough for the wild bush kids who didn't want to be there.

Beth fell in love with our very handsome stockman, Dave Mills, who was saving to buy his own cattle station. Dave loved bush poetry and rum, and was able to consume copious amounts of both. Beth and Dave were married on the front verandah of our house in August 1968 and I, aged twelve, was chosen to be one of the flower girls. This was one of the most exciting things that had ever happened to me! I had never seen a wedding and did not own a dress.

My measurements were sent off to some dressmaker in Brisbane and, lo and behold, just like magic, this piece of paper was transformed into the most beautiful fuchsia pink princess-line dress I had ever seen in my life. The dress came on the mail plane with Beth's full-length white lace dress with veil, silk bouquet and white high-heeled shoes. I felt like a princess and danced around on the dirt dance floor all night in my glorious dress with the white lace trim under the bodice, matching silk flower bouquet and a spray of flowers in my hair.

At the time of the wedding, unfortunately, we were in the midst of a nasty rat plague. These are not the type of creatures you invite to a wedding. I don't know why there were millions of fat, grey rats invading the country but I do know that they ate everything in their path, including my beautiful pink dress. The morning after the wedding, I picked my dress up from beside the bed and it had raggedy holes chewed right into the front of it. I was devastated. I had dreamt of wearing it to every party on the station for the rest of my life!

Our little school eventually received cement floors, doors and louvred windows. By the end of my primary schooling, Billy and I shared the classroom with our younger siblings Shing, Sam and Joe, and some of the young Aboriginal children.

I did Grade 8 by correspondence before being told at the end of 1969 that Billy and I would be sent to boarding school the following year. I found it difficult learning subjects like science from a page and languages like Latin and French were worlds away from what I was living and experiencing. Most of it made no sense at all. I was far better at speaking Mudburra, the local Indigenous language. Grade 8 by correspondence had not been very successful, so I was to repeat the year down south.

All the time that I was being home schooled, there was still work to do. It was a different kind of education, I suppose. I'd do anything that needed doing, because everyone worked on Killarney, regardless of age. I'd work in the cattle yards, helping with the drafting and branding. I'd go out on musters. I'd clean the houses, and look after the kids, just as I always had.

I loved being busy, loved helping the adults with the many tasks that had to be done. I wanted to be like the adults – they were our role models. They were people who worked hard and lived passionately; people who kept a community going and who cared about each other. We never for a second felt like we weren't valued or that we didn't have an important role to play. Maybe that was part of the genius of the way Bill Tapp and Mum ran the place: everyone felt like they belonged, everyone felt like they were worth something. It could be a difficult place – the seasons alone saw to that – but it was a place where everyone lived life fully. Not many kids get to grow up like that.

And I wasn't really looking forward to leaving that life behind to move down south for school.

24 Boarding School Days

I had just turned fourteen when I left the Northern Territory for school down in Queensland. Bill Tapp's mother, Sarah Tapp, had retired to the Gold Coast so it was decided that Billy and I would go to the coeducational school of Scots College and Presbyterian Girls College (PGC) in Warwick. We were waved off to boarding school on a road-train full of wild bulls and virtually empty suitcases, as we didn't have any clothing that would be suitable for the flash city life, and we didn't own things such as pyjamas, socks, or any winter gear. This would all be purchased on arrival at school along with uniforms and other essentials.

The road-train driver delivered us and the load of cattle to Darwin some twelve hours later, and we caught a plane directly to Brisbane. We had travelled on the mail plane on the odd occasion when going to school in Darwin; however, we had never been on a big passenger aeroplane, nor had we ever stayed in a nice motel room.

On the plane trip, Billy and I thought we were so sophisticated when we were handed a meal in a white glass dish with shiny stainless-steel knives and forks, linen serviettes and china teacups and saucers. Those were the days when real crockery and cutlery were standard on the aircraft, and most of the adults smoked on board.

We lifted the lid off the meal and after discussion about what some of the vegetables could possibly be, and who was game to try them first, we decided that we knew what the purple grape in the side salad was. We both popped the grape into our mouths at the same time. We spluttered and winced and looked at each other in disgust. It was a salty, sour olive. It took me many years to try one again and Billy still will not eat them.

A work colleague of Bill Tapp's picked us up at the airport and took us to a hotel in the middle of Brisbane. Our heads swivelled like the clowns in a sideshow alley as we drove through the city. Thousands of cars whizzed by and there were traffic lights and traffic jams, high-rise buildings and dazzling shop fronts and millions of white people.

We had never eaten in a restaurant or even a cafe until that night. Billy and I sat in the motel restaurant, wide eyed, as the waiter took our orders. We ordered steak and vegetables because we had no idea what half the things on the menu were. In 1970, Katherine, the closest town to Killarney, had a population of 2500 and no one there even owned a television.

The following day our grandmother picked us up from the hotel in her little silver Volkswagen and took us to the Gold Coast for the weekend. She couldn't wait to get us into a good hot bath and buy us some new clothes.

I felt very awkward and uncomfortable at my grandmother's. Having spent most of my life until then in a swag, I was overwhelmed by the beautiful bedroom she'd prepared for me, with crisp white cotton sheets and a floral bedspread. Delicate lace doilies sat beneath exquisite porcelain figurines and a Tiffany bedside lamp. I'd only ever seen such things in books. I crept carefully between the sheets with my crusty brown feet, wearing the first pair of pyjamas I had ever owned. I'd never slept in a room by myself, without my family close around me.

My little world was expanding rapidly and nothing prepared me for the homesickness, for feeling like a giant fish out of water in those first months at my new school. Everything was so foreign. I didn't talk much, I just did as I was told. As I was fitted out with a name tag and bottle-green school bag full of books, I wondered how I could get out of there and get home. Tears sat under my eyelids and I felt so lonely and out of my depth. I couldn't fathom the strictness and routine; the idea of having to wear uniforms with the hem exactly two inches below the knee and long brown socks pulled up to my knees were only two of the strange things required of me.

The bells echoed through the old wooden boarding house to get up in the morning, to go to breakfast, to catch the bus, to go to sport, to eat dinner and to do homework, and to go to bed. I hated those bells. The summer uniform was a blue-green tartan cotton shift with a woven panama hat. There were black shoes that had to be polished every afternoon. On Sundays, we had to walk the few blocks to the Presbyterian Church in our white linen suits, stockings, black shoes and panama hats.

This was the first year that PGC and Scots had amalgamated as a coeducational school and all lessons were held at Scots College. I couldn't wait to go over to Scots for lessons each day so I could see Billy and feel some connection to home. Our school also went over to Scots for socials, movies and sports days, so there were other opportunities to see the brother I was so used to seeing all the time, every day.

The first term ticked away like each day was forty-eight hours long. I cried on my bed every afternoon and sobbed with a pillow over my head far into the night. I walked over to meals in the dining room, where I was allocated a seat at a long, white linen-covered table, with a Year 12 Senior and a housemistress. I didn't know what cutlery to use and ate very little in those first weeks as I watched from under lowered lids to see how people ate. The food was foreign and I hated sago and porridge, but loved the fresh bread, butter and honey. I craved a big juicy steak, salty corned beef and rib bones cooked on the open fire.

I missed Killarney so much it was physical. The first three months of first term felt like three years. I eagerly waited for the long letters from my mum, who wrote in depth about what everyone at home was doing, how many cattle were mustered, whose birthday it was and who had been sick, or who'd had a fight and left the station. I loved letter-writing time on Saturday morning when I could write home and tell my mum how much I hated school and how I had to get out of there before I died of unhappiness!

The first school holidays finally arrived and as Billy and I flew into Darwin, looking at the stunning, flat, dry season landscape out of the plane window, I felt the weight of sadness lift off my chest. I could not wait to see my cousins and aunty in Darwin and my nana in Katherine on the way home.

In the car, every mile seemed to take forever, but we chattered excitedly as the landmarks flew by the window and finally the signpost came into view: KILLARNEY 42.

Then we were home; we knew every inch of that winding dirt track and were happy to open the five gates, the ones that we had fought over before boarding school days because no one ever wanted to open them.

As the station came into view, I cried with happiness and swore I was never leaving again, no matter what Mum or Bill Tapp said.

We jumped out of the car into the house – 'Hello, Mum, we're home.' We threw our cases on the beds and headed up to the cattle yards to see everyone and to make sure everything else was the same. Bill Tapp was still in the office on the phone, Mum still had a tea towel over her shoulder and a cigarette in her hand. There was our Aboriginal house help, Nancy Holtze, hanging out the washing, and kids running in and out of the house, just as they always did.

The dust still hung thick over the cattle yards as the cattle bawled and the stockmen banged gates and slammed the red branding iron. My horse was still there and my saddle was hanging where it always hung.

Old Micko was still in the kitchen, the handsome young stockmen were still laughing, teasing and skylarking, and the old women were still at the camp. I felt like I had gone to heaven. My home hadn't disappeared while I was living in another part of the universe.

That night we had a family dinner at home, all eight children and Mum and Bill Tapp, feasting on a bubbling beef stew and heaps of mashed potato as we laughed and I bragged about school and how we had to wear pyjamas and dressing gowns and socks, and ribbons in our hair.

Billy and I filled the days with working in the yards, riding with cattle, drafting and branding, and swimming in the muddy dams. We ate in the men's dining room and sat outside at night, catching up on all the stories, playing guitars and singing country and western songs.

Billy and I reluctantly headed back to school after the holidays finished and I lasted there for another four years, making many friends and growing to enjoy some of the activities, like dancing and joining the school magazine committee, singing in the choir and diving.

My brother Daniel was born in 1971. Mum timed it well because I was home on school holidays. Her final and tenth child, Kate, was born in December 1973, a few weeks after I had finished school in Year 11. Daniel and Kate were both born during the Wet so there was the worry that an uncrossable swollen river or getting bogged could mean the baby being born on the side of the road. Somehow luck was always on their side and Mum made it to hospital in time.

That final wet season school holidays, when Kate was born, I was able to convince Bill Tapp that I would be more use at home working than returning to Queensland for Year 12. While most of my friends seemed to know what careers they would follow when they left school, the only thing I knew was that I wanted to be home where I truly belonged, with my family on Killarney cattle station.

25 Killarney Now

Killarney grew larger and larger and was a very successful cattle station in the 1970s and 1980s. Unfortunately, circumstances changed and by the early 1990s our family no longer owned it. In 2014 it was sold to a large Australian pastoral company for a reported 35 million dollars.

I've spent many years away from Killarney now. I married and moved to another cattle station and raised my own children there.

You might think I would miss the home of my childhood, but I don't, because it is always in me. The red dirt, the heat, the magnificent dry seasons, the lush rains of the wet season; the songs of Slim Dusty or of Old Dora and Old Daisy; Micko's cakes, sugar-bag and johnnycakes; the imaginary footprint of a debil debil. The swaying movement of thousands of cattle streaming down the fence line towards the yards, the smell of the dust and the branding iron, and of rib bones cooking on coals. These memories will never leave me.

My brothers and sisters tearing around the homestead, my mother's wild intelligence and flashing eyes, Bill Tapp's dark, penetrating gaze and his mighty dream fill my heart with love and appreciation.

Killarney shaped who I am. There's nothing I would change about the years I spent growing up on the station. My Outback childhood was full of love, fun, danger and adventures, as I reckon every kid's life should be.

Glossary

agribusiness – a business that is involved in the production, distribution and sale of agricultural produce.
anvil – a heavy iron block onto which hot metals are hammered into shape.
aquifer – an underground layer of water-bearing rock. Water-bearing rocks are permeable, meaning that they have openings that liquids and gases can pass through.
billycan – a container for boiling water or making tea.
bore – a deep hole of small diameter bored to the aquifer of an artesian basin to get water.
bough shed – a simple shed made with four wooden posts, using tree branches for a roof.
branding – a mark made by burning or otherwise to indicate ownership of an animal.
breaking a horse – to train to obedience; tame.

caliper – an appliance used on limbs to provide extra support or to fix deformities.

coolamon – a shovel-shaped small tree trunk carved from the stinkwood tree, used to carry everything from firewood to food and babies.

corroboree – an Aboriginal assembly of sacred, festive or warlike dance.

dam – a female parent of a horse.

debil debil – word used for ghosts and devils.

droving – to herd cattle or sheep and drive them over long distances.

dysentery – an infectious stomach virus that leads to severe diarrhoea.

feral or bush cattle – cattle that range wild and untended in the bush.

gallon – a measurement in the Imperial system for capacity. One gallon of liquid equals 3.785 litres.

Gurindji – a group of Indigenous Australians living in northern Australia, 460 km southwest of Katherine in the Northern Territory's Victoria River region.

humpy – a temporary bush shelter used by Indigenous Australians.

jackaroo – a young man who works on a cattle station, to gain practical experience in the skills needed to become an owner, overseer or manager.

johnnycakes – a small flat damper of wheatmeal or flour about as big as the palm of the hand, cooked on both sides often on top of the embers of a campfire.

killer – a cow or bull that is slaughtered to feed the workers on a property.

lancewood – a hardy tree with a straight trunk used to build cattle yards.

long drop – a pit toilet.

Mudburra – a group of Indigenous Australians living in northern Australia.

mule – the offspring of a male donkey and a mare (a female horse).

muster – to round up cattle for sorting and/or branding.

nulla nulla – an Aboriginal club or heavy weapon.

pannikin – a small enamel cup.

pastoralist – a person who owns and manages sheep or cattle on a property.

sapper – a soldier who performs combat engineering duties such as building roads and repairing bridges.

sire – a male parent of a horse.

smoko – a break from work, perhaps for a cup of tea or a cigarette.

Stolen Generation – generations of Indigenous children who were removed from their families and communities, by government or non-government agencies, in order to enforce integration into white society.

sugar-bag – wild golden honey.

telephonist – a person who worked on the telephone exchange, connecting calls manually.

ten-gallon hat – a cowboy's broad-brimmed hat with a high, soft crown.

weevil – a small beetle that is considered a pest because it gets into stored flour and eats it.

woomera – a type of throwing stick with a notch at one end for holding a dart or spear.

Acknowledgements

I always wanted to write a book about my childhood because I knew that it was very different to how most Australians grew up. Achieving that dream cannot be done without a group of people who understand that dream and support you.

First and foremost, I thank my wonderful publisher Sophie Hamley who recognised and believed in my story way back in 2014 and has travelled this journey with me to publish three books, *A Sunburnt Childhood*, *My Outback Life* and now the children's version, *My Outback Childhood*. Thank you to the team at Hachette Australia, Karen Ward and Brigid Mullane. You are all a joy to work with.

Thank you to my dear friends in the Katherine Region of Writers (KROW) Royelene Hill, Jill Pettigrew, Kathleen Donald, Bruce Hocking, Lyndal Carbery and Christina

Allgood who have taken on many writing challenges and published a suite of anthologies over the past 27 years, always supporting and encouraging each other through our individual journeys.

I would like to dedicate this book to the people of the Outback; the mothers and home tutors who teach their children through School of the Air and Distance Education Schools. I am privileged to know so many of these wonderful families who put the high financial cost and commitment of their children's education first. And to the members of the Isolated Children's Parents Association (ICPA) who go in fighting loud and proud, year after year, for equality and equity to education for kids in the bush.